The Colors of Fall
Road Trip Guide

Jerry and Marcy Monkman

The Countryman Press
Woodstock, Vermont

The Colors of Fall Road Trip Guide

ISBN 978-0-88150-869-7

Maps by Paul Woodward, © The Countryman Press
Book design and composition by S. E. Livingston

Published by The Countryman Press,
P.O. Box 748, Woodstock, VT 05091
Distributed by W. W. Norton & Company, Inc.,
500 Fifth Avenue, New York, NY 10110

Printed in China

10 9 8 7 6 5 4 3 2 1

CONTENTS

Introduction 5

I. UP NORTH, WAY NORTH

1. Vermont's Northeast Kingdom I:
   St. Johnsbury, Burke, and the Connecticut River 11
2. Vermont's Northeast Kingdom II: Groton State Forest, Cabot, and Peacham........17
3. North of the White Mountains: Dixville Notch and Stark 21
4. Maine's Big Woods: The Kennebec Valley and Moosehead Lake 27
5. Maine's Rangeley Lake Region.....................................33

II. APPALACHIAN VISTAS

6. Classic White Mountains Tour: Crawford and Franconia Notches..................39
7. Vermont's Smugglers' Notch 47
8. Vermont Route 100 Mountain Gaps 51
9. Maine's Grafton Notch...57
10. Massachusetts's High Point: Mount Greylock 61
11. The Mohawk Trail: Historic Massachusetts Highway 67
12. Western Connecticut Highlands: The Litchfield Hills 73

III. RURAL NEW ENGLAND LANDSCAPES

13. Southern Vermont Odyssey: Classic Villages and Back Roads 79
14. New Hampshire's Mount Monadnock 83
15. Covered Bridge Tour: Southwestern New Hampshire.................87
16. Connecticut River Upper Valley: New Hampshire and Vermont 93
17. New Hampshire's Lakes Region 99
18. Maine's Western Lakes Region....................................105
19. Southern Berkshires: Hay Fields, Waterfalls, and Cobbles 109
20. Pioneer Valley Vistas: Massachusetts's Connecticut River Tour 115
21. Not Far from Boston: Central Massachusetts 119

IV. COASTAL BYWAYS

22. Acadia National Park Loop Road 125
23. Maine's Midcoast: Wiscasset to Camden 129
24. Rhode Island Beaches and Mansions: Westerly to Newport 135
25. Historic Seacoast: Newburyport, Massachusetts, to Ogunquit, Maine 139

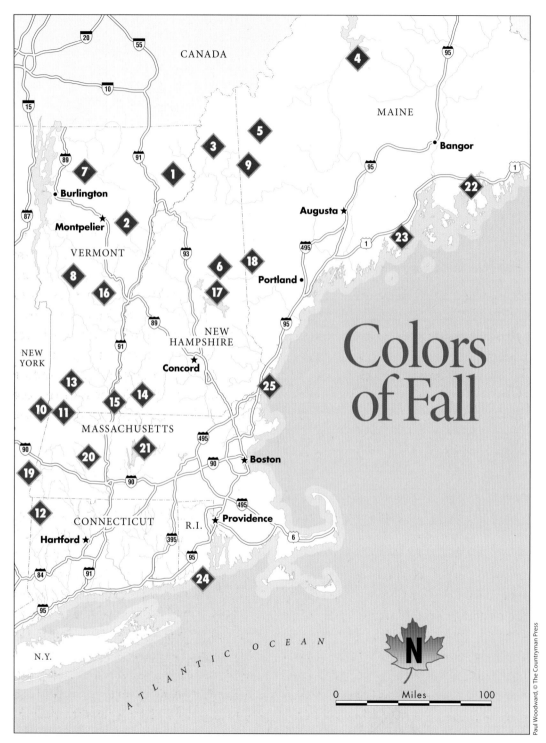

INTRODUCTION

For those who love the outdoors and the aesthetics of rural landscapes, fall in New England is the high point of the year. The world explodes in color, and senses awaken to a rich natural variety, from cool misty forests to the warmth of sun-soaked fields and orchards. Of course, something so sublime is often fleeting, and this peak moment of our temperate weather cycle is short, lasting a few weeks at most before cold and snow quiet the forests, fields, and village centers. We have been reveling in and photographing fall in New England since we moved here from the Midwest more than twenty years ago. Despite these twenty-plus years of immersing ourselves in the autumn landscape, we continue to be excited every year by the prospect of creating new images that capture the essence of the region's beauty and convey the meaning of the changing colors of its maples, birches, and oaks.

In 2003 we published a small book of photos titled *The Colors of Fall,* a collection of some of our favorite images of autumn in New England. This celebration of the season has proven to be popular year after year as visitors flock to the region. Readers are always curious to know exactly where we took our photos. Their questions inspired this book. In writing it we revisited favorite places and traveled to new destinations that had been on our to-do list for years. We admit that this was a pretty great job to have for a couple of months, and we wish you as much enjoyment as you use this guide in charting your own fall foliage travels.

The New England Foliage Season: What to Expect

Timing. Timing a fall foliage visit is easy, as long as you realize that nature doesn't always follow exact schedules. Columbus Day weekend in October is the traditional "peak" weekend for leaf peeping. Visitors are pretty much guaranteed there will be peak color somewhere in New England at this time, but exactly where is anyone's guess. In general, leaves start turning first in the hills and mountains of northern New England in late September, peaking around the first week of October, with the color gradually moving south and toward the coast throughout the month. Higher elevations peak before lower elevations, with the exception of freshwater wetlands dominated by red maples. By November 1, the show is over in all but the warmest pockets of coastal oak-hickory forests. To help you plan your visit, we have listed the typical peak foliage time at the beginning of each trip description.

Color. The fall foliage for which New England is famous is found in the hardwood forests of northern New England and in the hills of western Massachusetts. These forests are dominated by sugar maples, American beech, and yellow birch, which combine to make a beautiful mix of orange, yellow, and bronze colors. The occasional red maple adds the splashes of red that get people really excited, though depending on weather and soil conditions, sugar maples will turn red as well.

At higher mountain elevations, the forest is dominated by paper birch trees, which turn a brilliant yellow and are usually complemented by the dark greens of spruce and fir trees. In southern and coastal areas, you will still find pockets of northern hardwoods, but oak-hickory forests are more dominant. The color displayed in these forests is less gaudy than up north, being primarily yellow and russet, with some of the oaks turning red in

good foliage years. Also, don't overlook the color in the coastal salt marshes. As the salt hay turns from green to brown it can take on varying shades of brown, red, and gold, offering vistas that are just as visually pleasing as the bigger forest displays.

Weather. Fall is a time of change, and that obviously applies to the weather as well. Average daytime temperatures are in the 50s and 60s (Fahrenheit), but it is just as common to have days in the 40s or the 70s. Night can bring temperatures as low as the 20s, especially in northern New England. Rain, fog, and drizzle are common throughout the fall season, and snow is possible as well, even in early October. However, sunny days are also typical. Basically, you need to be prepared for just about any weather.

Lodging. This guide does not include lodging suggestions, but we can make one observation that holds true year after year: expect lodging rates to be as high or higher in the fall than at any other time of the year, as foliage season is one of the most popular times to visit the region. Rates at some hotels are a little lower during the week, but if you plan on visiting during a weekend, make advance reservations and plan to pay a premium. Campground reservations should be made well ahead of time for a fall weekend visit. If you are traveling after Columbus Day, be advised that some establishments in the region shut down for the winter months; call ahead when making travel plans.

Traffic. In general, you will rarely encounter traffic problems if your leaf-peeping excursions take place on weekdays. However, certain routes can get very busy during fall weekends. In particular, you can expect a lot of company during peak weekends on the Kancamagus Highway (Trip 6), VT 100 in the Green Mountains (Trip 8), and the Park Loop Road in Acadia National Park (Trip 22).

Using This Guide

The 25 trips included in this book range in length from an 18-mile drive through Vermont's Smugglers' Notch to a 145-mile journey in Maine's North Woods. Where relevant, trip descriptions will alert readers to unpaved or gravel roads, but in general all of the driving routes mentioned herein are accessible to passenger vehicles. In general, travelers will end up spending half a day to a full day exploring each route. The trips outlined here are intended as suggestions. Each offers an excellent way to spend a day enjoying the fall colors. Travelers are expected to make their own adaptations, according to personal interests.

When using this guide, keep in mind the following:

Mileage. The mileage listed at the beginning of each trip is the approximate length of the drive outlined on the accompanying map. We feel the mileages in the text are accurate, but some are approximations and may vary slightly from the mileage your own vehicle measures.

Driving Times. The driving times listed at the beginning of each trip reflect the time it takes to drive the outlined routes without stopping. Your own travel time will vary depending on how much time you spend along the way.

Services. Since most of the trips outlined in this book are in rural areas, we have listed the places along each route that offer the most services. On some trips, these are large towns with a full complement of stores, restaurants, gas stations, et cetera. For the more out-of-the-way destinations, services might be limited to a gas station and/or general store.

Fees. For each trip, we have listed any entrance fees to parks and roads that we consider integral parts of the route. Generally, any fees associated with visiting cities or parks not specifically outlined in the trip discussions have not been included.

Hot Spots. For each trip, we have highlighted a few stops along the way that we feel are worth your time because of their scenic beauty or cultural value. We don't like spending the whole day in the car, and we're guessing you don't either. Here we invite you to pull over, get some fresh air, and maybe snap a few photos. We've also included a few optional side trips for those with the time and inclination to extend their travels.

Leg Stretchers. Not surprisingly given the location, the trips listed in this guide offer a variety of hiking and walking opportunities. Some are mentioned in the trip descriptions, but many appear in sidebars as destinations unto themselves. These range from short one- or two-hour rambles to adventurous, challenging hikes. Plan ahead for these excursions: bring energy snacks and water, and allow for an appropriate amount of time on the trail.

⦿ **GPS coordinates.** Although GPS technology is certainly not necessary in following this guide, for the benefit of readers so equipped, we have included GPS coordinates for all starting and ending locations, as well as hot spots along the way. These coordinates are in degree/minute/decimal-minute format—be sure to account for this format if you use these figures for navigation purposes. Also, please use common sense in employing this technology and always heed the map and trip descriptions when following these routes.

PART I

Up North, Way North

Fall colors, The Forks, Maine.

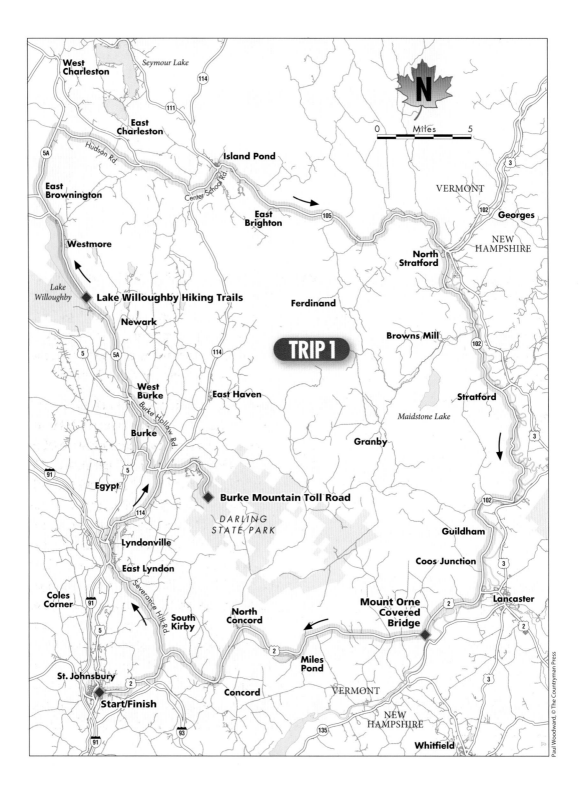

West Charleston

Seymour Lake

114

111

East Charleston

5A

Hudson Rd.

Island Pond

Center School Rd.

East Browning

Westmore

Lake Willoughby

◆ Lake Willoughby Hiking Trails

Newark

East Brighton

105

VERMONT

102

Georges

NEW HAMPSHIRE

North Stratford

Ferdinand

Browns Mill

5

5A

114

West Burke

Burke Hollow Rd.

East Haven

TRIP 1

Stratford

102

Maidstone Lake

91

Burke

5

Egypt

114

◆ Burke Mountain Toll Road

DARLING STATE PARK

Granby

3

Guildham

3

Lyndonville

East Lyndon

Coos Junction

3

Coles Corner

91

Severance Hill Rd.

5

South Kirby

North Concord

Mount Orne Covered Bridge ◆

2

Lancaster

2

St. Johnsbury

2

◆ Start/Finish

2

Miles Pond

3

Concord

VERMONT

93

135

NEW HAMPSHIRE

91

Whitfield

0 Miles 5

N

VERMONT

102

Paul Woodward, © The Countryman Press

Vermont's Northeast Kingdom I: St. Johnsbury, Burke, and the Connecticut River

The Trip: Plan to spend most of the day on this 125-mile loop in the beautiful hills and forests of Vermont's Northeast Kingdom. Except for in the little cities of St. Johnsbury and Lyndonville, this drive involves long stretches through scenic countryside and forests, interrupted only briefly by the occasional small village. There are expansive views of the entire region from the summit of Burke Mountain, reached via

> **Distance**
> 125 miles round-trip
> **Approximate Driving Time**
> 3 hours 30 minutes
> **Peak Time**
> Last week of September and first week of October
> **Services**
> St. Johnsbury, Lyndonville, East Burke, Island Pond
> **Fees**
> $5.00 per vehicle for Burke Mountain toll road

toll road, as well as intimate views of fall foliage along river and farm roads. The leaves turn here a little earlier than in most of New England, with good color starting at the end of September and peaking some time during the first week of October.

Basic Route: This trip follows US 2 east from St. Johnsbury to Severance Hill Road, a scenic back road that leads north to US 5 in Lyndonville via Red Village Road. Follow US 5 north through Lyndonville to VT 114 east, which leads 5 miles to Mountain Road, the toll road up Burke Mountain. Coming back from Burke Mountain, follow VT 114 west for 0.3 mile to Burke Hollow Road, which winds its way north through farm country to VT 5A, which will take you north past the cliffs of Lake Willoughby to Hudson Road east to VT 105. Follow VT 105 east to VT 102 south, which parallels the scenic Connecticut River for another 23 miles. In Guildhall, turn left and follow US 2 west back to St. Johnsbury.

Start: US 2 and US 5 in St. Johnsbury, Vermont. "St. J" has a vibrant downtown with shops and restaurants on Railroad Street, and two museums worth visiting—the Athenaeum and the Fairbanks Museum, both on Main Street. To begin the drive, go east on US 2, crossing the Passumpsic River and heading toward Concord.

◉ **GPS coordinates:**
N 44 25.159, W 72 0.934.

Five miles east of St. Johnsbury, turn left onto Severance Hill Road, which passes through quiet farm country for 4.7 miles to Red Village Road. Turn left here for the 1.6-mile drive to US 5 north in Lyndonville. At the north end of town, turn right on VT 114 toward Burke.

Hot Spot: Burke Mountain toll road. About 4.5 miles east of US 5 is the little ski village of East Burke, known both for the ski area and Kingdom Trails, the mecca of New England mountain biking. Just past the center of town, turn right on Mountain Road, bearing left onto the toll road in about 2 miles ($5 fee). The toll road follows switchbacks up past several viewpoints to a parking area just below the summit of Burke Mountain. There are good views to the north from the parking area, but even better views from the fire tower, which is a short 10-minute hike from the parking lot.

◉ **GPS coordinates:**
N 44 34.253, W 71 53.664.

Head back down the mountain to VT 114 and turn left, then right in 0.3 mile onto Burke Hollow Road for a 5-mile drive through rural Vermont countryside to VT 5A north in West Burke.

Hot Spot: Lake Willoughby. A little over 6 miles north of Burke Hollow Road, you will reach the south end of Lake Willoughby, a narrow 5-mile-long body of water that is popular with the summer crowd. This is the most dramatic scenery of the trip, as the south end of the lake squeezes through the cliffs of Mount Pisgah and Mount Hor, which tower more than 1,000 feet above the surface of the lake. Because of these cliffs, the southern end of the lake is generally wild and undeveloped, making it a great place to canoe or kayak. You can also hike to the tops of the cliffs for a dizzying view of the lake (see "Mount Willoughby Leg Stretchers").

◉ **GPS coordinates:**
N 44 43.031, W 72 1.809.

VT 5A continues past the lake to Hudson Road (10 miles north of the southern end of Lake Willoughby). Turn right on Hudson, which is a gravel road that makes for possibly the flattest 5-mile drive in the entire Northeast Kingdom. For most of its length, it passes through wide-open farm country, with views extending to the horizon in all directions. At the end of Hudson Road, turn right onto VT 105 east for the 21-mile drive through the little town of Island Pond and the wild Nulhegan River valley to VT 102 in Bloomfield.

In Bloomfield, follow VT 102 south for a meandering 23-mile drive along a stretch of the Connecticut River that is rife with twists and oxbows. For much of the drive, the road is up high on the western bank of the river, providing views across farms and the river to the mountains in New Hampshire. VT 102 ends at the town green in Guildhall and its picturesque whitewashed churches and town buildings. Turn right

Farm on the Connecticut River near Guildhall, Vermont, framed by the yellow leaves of a silver maple.

🔺 Hay bales, East Burke, Vermont.

here to follow US 2 west through another scenic village, Lunenburg, on the way back to St. Johnsbury.

Hot Spot: Mt. Orne Covered Bridge. About 4 miles west of Guildhall, bear left onto River Road (aka Town Highway 1) for a 0.3-mile side trip to the Mt. Orne Covered Bridge. Built in 1911 to replace an ear-

lier bridge destroyed by a logjam in 1908, this 266-foot-long bridge spans the Connecticut River, connecting Lunenburg, Vermont, with Lancaster, New Hampshire. There are nice views of the bridge and mountains from the east side of the river.

⦿ **GPS coordinates:** N 44 27.616, W 71 39.193.

Mount Willoughby Leg Stretchers

Several trails in the area lead to various viewpoints from the cliffs on both sides of the lake. We've listed two here—a short climb to a viewpoint on the lower part of the cliffs on Mount Hor, and a longer trip to the summit of Mount Pisgah. For more detailed descriptions of these and other hikes in the area, check out the Green Mountain Club's *Day Hiker's Guide to Vermont*.

South Shore Trail. This trail starts from the parking area on the left side of the road at the south end of the lake. It follows a rough trail at moderate grades, climbing 150 feet in 1.3 miles to views of the lake from below the cliffs of Mount Hor. Average hiking time is 40 minutes each way.

⦿ **GPS coordinates:**
N 44 43.031, W 72 1.809.

South Trail. If you're after the dizzying views mentioned in the trip description, this is the hike for you. The South Trail begins from a parking area on the right side of VT 5A, 0.4 mile south of Lake Willoughby. The trail alternates between steep and moderate gains as it climbs 1,450 feet over the 1.7 miles between the trailhead and the summit. It passes two dramatic views before reaching the peak, and there is a third

🔺 Cliffs of Mount Pisgah above Lake Willoughby.

great lookout, 0.3 miles beyond the summit on the North Trail.

⦿ **GPS coordinates:**
N 44 42.640, W 72 1.453.

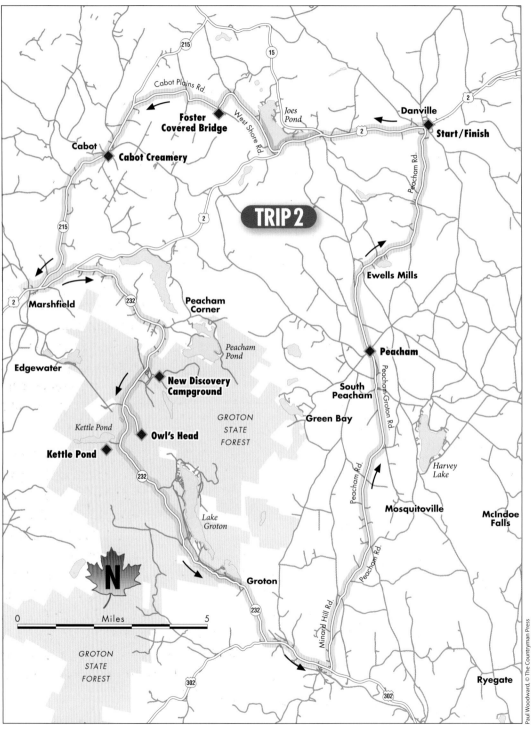

215

15

Cabot Plains Rd.

Joes
Pond

2

Danville

**Foster
Covered Bridge**

West Shore Rd.

Start/Finish

Cabot

Cabot Creamery

Peacham Rd.

2

215

TRIP 2

Ewells Mills

2

Marshfield

232

Peacham
Corner

Peacham
Pond

Peacham-Groton Rd.

Peacham

Edgewater

**New Discovery
Campground**

South
Peacham

Kettle Pond

Owl's Head

GROTON
STATE
FOREST

Green Bay

Harvey
Lake

Peacham Rd.

Kettle Pond

232

Lake
Groton

Mosquitoville

McIndoe
Falls

Peacham Rd.

N

Groton

232

GROTON
STATE
FOREST

Minard Hill Rd.

0   Miles   5

302

Ryegate

302

Paul Woodward, © The Countryman Press

Vermont's Northeast Kingdom II: Groton State Forest, Cabot, and Peacham

The Trip: This 50-mile loop features a little bit of everything that is Vermont: rolling hillsides dotted with cows, a covered bridge, remote forests, and white steepled churches. It begins and ends in a small village on US 2 (Danville) and negotiates rural paved and dirt roads past even smaller towns (Cabot, Groton, and Peacham). While most of the drive through this pastoral scenery is far from civilization, you will feel even further removed on VT 232 through Groton State Forest. Here you will drive for several miles without seeing a man-made structure of any kind. During peak foliage, the road is awash with color. The more open landscapes of this trip are also great in the fall, with fields, barns, and churches set against a backdrop of colorful hillsides. Though it's only 50 miles long, give yourself three or four hours to really enjoy this drive.

Basic Route: This trip follows US 2 west from Danville to West Shore Road just past Joe's Pond, and then follows Cabot Plains Road for about 3 miles through fields and farms before reaching VT 215 just north of Cabot Village. It then follows VT 215 south for 6 miles through Cabot to US 2 for a short 1-mile jaunt east to VT 232. VT 232 stretches for 13.5 miles through the Groton State Forest to US 302. Take US 302 east for 2 miles to Peacham Road on the left, which leads 15.5 miles back to Danville and US 2.

Distance
50 miles round-trip
Approximate Driving Time
1 hour 30 minutes
Peak Time
First and second weeks of October
Services
Small amount in Danville, Marshfield, Groton. More in St. Johnsbury, 10 miles east of Danville.
Fees
None

△ Rainbow over farmland, Peacham, Vermont.

Start: US 2 and Peacham Road in Danville, Vermont. You'll find a town green with a white gazebo and church, and a few storefronts. Danville is the picture of a Vermont small town. To begin the drive, head west on US 2.

◉ **GPS coordinates:**
N 44 24.690, W 72 8.405.

At 4.3 miles west of Danville, turn right on West Shore Road and follow it for 2 miles to Cabot Plains Road; turn left.

Hot Spot: Foster Covered Bridge. After about 1.5 miles, Cabot Plains Road hits a T intersection; turn right. Just after this turn you will see the Foster Covered Bridge set about 100 yards off the road in a field on the left. The bridge is on private property, but it's OK to walk down and check it out. It's small and nondescript, but somewhat unique sitting out in the field by itself, near the top of a hill with views of farms and hills stretching for miles.

◉ **GPS coordinates:**
N 44 25.401, W 72 16.091.

After the bridge, take the road to the left to VT 215 (Main Street), about 3 miles west of West Shore Road. Follow VT 215 south (left) through the center of Cabot and past the Cabot Creamery (stop here at the visitor center for a cheese-making tour—$2) for 6 miles back to US 2 east; turn left. A little over a mile east of VT 215, turn right on VT 232 toward the Groton State Forest.

Hot Spot: Groton State Forest. A couple of miles south of US 2, you will enter the state forest as the road narrows and the landscape changes from rural farmland to deep woods. There are several features in the forest worth checking out. Two of the best are Owl's Head peak and Kettle Pond. To get to Owl's Head, turn left on Lanesboro Road, 5.5 miles south of US 2. At the end of the road is a parking area and a 10-minute hike up to rock ledges with beautiful views of the forest and mountains to the south and west. Kettle Pond is on VT 232, another mile south of Lanesboro Road. A flat though sometimes muddy trail circumnavigates the pond, giving you an intimate view of the forest and its foliage.

◉ **GPS coordinates:**
N 44 17.888, W 72 17.634 (Owl's Head) and N 44 17.680, W 72 18.262 (Kettle Pond).

▼ Classic New England vista, Peacham, Vermont.

Groton State Park Leg Stretcher

In addition to the hikes to Owl's Head and Kettle Pond mentioned in the trip description, there are several hikes in Groton State Park that begin at the New Discovery Campground (on VT 232, 4.5 miles south of US 2). Two noteworthy rambles are the 1.8-mile loop around Osmore Pond and the hike up Big Deer Mountain (trail maps are available at the campground). The moderate hike up Big Deer Mountain climbs about 400 feet for 1.4 miles over the wooded summit to open ledges with beautiful views of Lake Groton. The hike should take about one and a half hours round-trip.

● **GPS coordinates:**
N 44 19.179, W 72 17.234.

Seven miles south of Kettle Pond, turn left onto US 302, then turn left on Peacham Road (aka Minard Hill Road) in 2 miles.

Hot Spot: Peacham. Like the roads in Cabot, Peacham Road meanders through rural Vermont at its best. About 9 miles north of US 302, you will come to the center of Peacham, where you will find a few houses and barns, a general store, and a classic New England church with a tall white steeple. The best view of the village is up the hill on Church Street in the field next to the firehouse. There are also nice views from the cemetery across the street, and from many locations on the various dirt roads in the surrounding countryside.

● **GPS coordinates:**
N 44 19.613, W 72 10.352.

To complete the trip, continue north on Peacham Road for another 7 miles to US 2 in Danville.

North of the White Mountains: Dixville Notch and Stark

The Trip: North of New Hampshire's White Mountains, the towns are small and spread out, and the spaces in between are filled with hilly wilderness where the forests are thick and wildlife like moose and black bears are common. This drive starts in Colebrook, near the banks of the Connecticut River, and makes a big 90-mile loop, passing impressive cliffs in Dixville Notch, the trout-filled whitewater of the Androscoggin River south of Errol, and the tiny town of Stark. Northern New Hampshire is a transition zone between the northern hardwood forests to the south and the spruce-fir forests to the north.

Distance
90 miles round-trip
Approximate Driving Time
2 hours 45 minutes
Peak Time
First week of October
Services
Colebrook, Errol, Groveton
Fees
$4 per adult for entrance to Milan Hill State Park

When fall colors are at their peak here, the reds, oranges, and yellows of the hardwood forests contrast sharply with evergreen groves of spruce, fir, and pine.

Basic Route: This trip starts and ends in Colebrook, heading east on NH 26 and south on NH 16 before looping back west and north on NH 110B, NH 110A, NH 110, and US 3.

Start and Finish: US 3 and NH 26 in Colebrook, New Hampshire. Colebrook is the biggest town in this part of New Hampshire, so this is the place to gas up and get provisioned for the trip. To start the drive, head east on NH 26 toward Dixville Notch.

◉ **GPS coordinates:**
N 44 53.572, W 71 29.833.

Hot Spot: Dixville Notch. The tiny hamlet of Dixville Notch, 10 miles west of Colebrook, is home to the Balsams Grand Resort and best known as the first place in the nation to cast its votes in the U.S. presidential election. The notch is small but dramatic, with 400-foot cliffs towering over

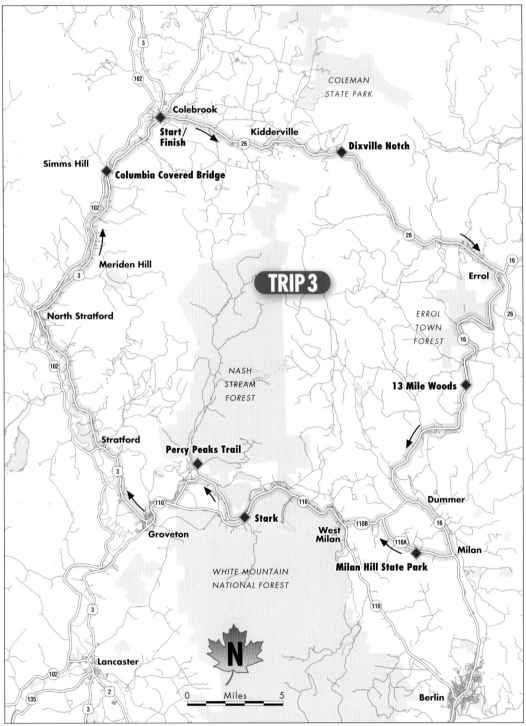

COLEMAN
STATE PARK

Colebrook

Start/
Finish

Kidderville

26

Dixville Notch

Simms Hill

Columbia Covered Bridge

102

26

16

Errol

Meriden Hill

3

TRIP 3

ERROL
TOWN
FOREST

26

16

North Stratford

102

NASH
STREAM
FOREST

13 Mile Woods

Stratford

3

Percy Peaks Trail

Dummer

110

110

16

110

West
Milan

110B

Stark

Groveton

Milan Hill State Park

110A

Milan

WHITE MOUNTAIN
NATIONAL FOREST

110

N

Lancaster

102

2

0   Miles   5

Berlin

135

3

Paul Woodward, © The Countryman Press

the road and Lake Gloriette. A handful of steep trails lead to overlooks on the rocky ledges, and there is also a pair of waterfalls worth visiting: Dixville Flume and Huntington Cascades. Trail maps are available at the Balsams.

◉ **GPS coordinates:**
N 44 51.977, W 71 18.141.

Eleven miles east of Dixville Notch is Errol, a small town that caters to outdoors enthusiasts, its location on the Androscoggin River next to Umbagog National Wildlife Refuge being the perfect jumping-off point for all kinds of recreational activities—fly-fishing, lake fishing, hunting, snowmobiling, camping, canoeing, white-water paddling, and moose watching. If you want to spend a few days in the great outdoors, this is the place to do it. At the intersection of NH 26 and NH 16, turn right on NH 16 south.

Hot Spot: 13-Mile Woods. South of Errol, NH 16 parallels the fast-flowing water of the Androscoggin River. Most of the 21-mile drive from Errol to Milan is undeveloped and crowded with moose, and this is your best opportunity to see these gentle giants of the North Woods. Moose are most active at dawn and dusk, but it is possible to see them at any time during the day.

◉ **GPS coordinates:**
N 44 43.031, W 71 10.398.

🔺 Dixville Notch.

Hot Spot: Milan Hill State Park. At 21.5 miles south of NH 26, turn right on NH 110B in Milan. In 2 miles, turn left into Milan Hill State Park. There is a campground in the park that includes a half-dozen new yurts, where you can spend the night warm and toasty next to a wood stove. You can also stop here and climb the lookout tower in the park for spectacular views of the White Mountains to the south and the Percy Peaks to the north.

◉ **GPS coordinates:**
N 44 34.329, W 71 13.385.

🔺 New Hampshire's Presidential Range as seen from Milan Hill State Park.

From Milan Hill, continue east on NH 110 B to its end, then turn left on NH 110A. In another 2.4 miles, turn right on NH 110.

Hot Spot: Stark Village. Seven miles west of NH 110A is the little village of Stark. The white steepled church and nearby covered bridge at the center of town make for possibly the most photographed scene in northern New Hampshire. Stark was named after the Revolutionary War general John Stark, who is credited with the "Live free or die" quote that became the state motto. The village of Stark was the home of a German POW camp during World War II. Today most people visit Stark to see the covered bridge and to hike in the nearby Nash Stream State Forest.

⦿ **GPS coordinates:**
N 44 36.044, W 71 24.463.

In Stark, turn right on Northside Road, crossing the bridge, then turn left to follow the Upper Ammonoosuc River as it flows west toward the Connecticut River. Northside Road passes fields with excellent views of the river and nearby mountains, and crosses Nash Stream, with views of the Percy Peaks, 4 miles west of the village. In another 0.7 miles beyond Nash Stream, turn left on Emerson Road and follow it for 1.5 miles back to NH 110; turn right.

In 2.5 miles, you will reach US 3 in Groveton, a small paper-mill town with another white covered bridge spanning the Upper Ammonoosuc. Turn right on US 3 north for a scenic drive with nice views of the Connecticut River and hillsides ablaze in fall color.

Hot Spot: Columbia Covered Bridge. About 22 miles north of Groveton, turn left on Columbia Bridge Road for a short drive to the Columbia Covered Bridge, which is the northernmost bridge on the Connecticut River connecting New Hampshire and Vermont. Built in 1912, the unpainted wooden bridge is 145 feet long.

⦿ **GPS coordinates:**
N 44 51.179, W 71 33.081.

From the Columbia bridge, it is another 4.2 miles north on US 3 back to Colebrook.

Percy Peaks Leg Stretcher

At nearly 40,000 acres in size, the Nash Stream State Forest near Stark offers some excellent hiking opportunities, with several peaks over 3,000 feet in elevation. The most conspicuous are a pair of rounded mountains called the Percy Peaks. The best views are from the bald top of North Percy Peak, where there are 360-degree views that stretch from the Canadian border south to the White Mountains. The best approach is via the Percy Peaks Trail, which climbs 2,200 feet in 2.2 miles to reach the summit, and is easy to follow—just be sure to stay on the orange-blazed Percy Peaks Trail when you reach an intersection with the Percy Loop Trail, about 0.5 mile below the summit. This is a strenuous hike that is steep for much of its length, so you should attempt it only in dry weather and only if you are in good physical condition. The up-and-back hike should take about three and a half hours. The trailhead is on the right side of Nash Stream Road, 2.7 miles north of Northside Road.

⦿ **GPS coordinates:**
N 44 39.933, W 71 27.455.

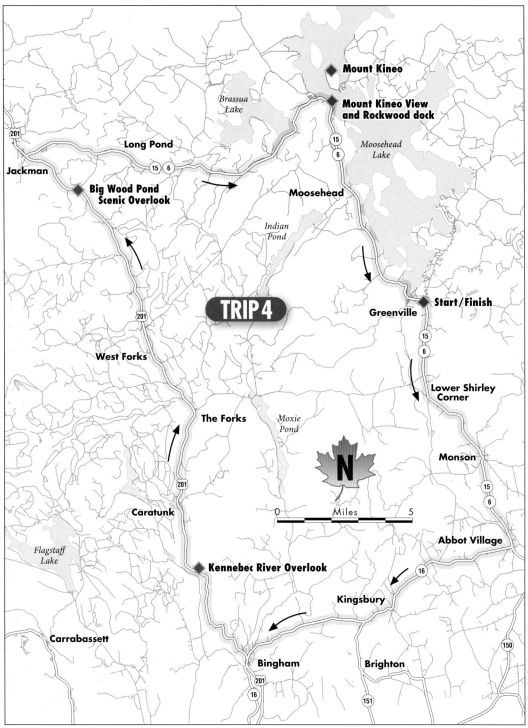

Mount Kineo

Mount Kineo View
and Rockwood dock

Brassua
Lake

Long Pond

15 6

15
6

Jackman

Big Wood Pond
Scenic Overlook

Moosehead

Moosehead
Lake

Indian
Pond

TRIP 4

201

Greenville

Start/Finish

15
6

West Forks

Lower Shirley
Corner

The Forks

Moxie
Pond

N

Monson

15
6

201

Caratunk

Miles

Abbot Village

16

Flagstaff
Lake

Kennebec River Overlook

Kingsbury

150

Carrabassett

Bingham

Brighton

201
16

151

Paul Woodward. © The Countryman Press

Maine's Big Woods: The Kennebec Valley and Moosehead Lake

The Trip: North of the 45th parallel in Maine lies the biggest forest in the eastern United States. There are close to 20 million acres of undeveloped land in Maine's North Woods, interrupted only occasionally by small villages. The majority of this land is managed as private timberland and thus is actively logged, but the region is still wild and beautiful, with sparkling sky-blue lakes reflecting rugged mountain ranges and lush forests. During fall, this trip takes you past some of the best foliage

views in Maine, on roads where moose are almost as common as people. At the southern tip of Moosehead Lake is Greenville, the biggest town in the area and a great place to start and end this drive, which explores the beauty of the Kennebec River valley, one of Maine's biggest watersheds. This trip includes long stretches where there are no towns, and small villages with no services, so stock up in Greenville. The drive takes nearly four hours nonstop, so give yourself at least six hours with food and other breaks.

Basic Route: This trip starts and ends in Greenville, heading south on ME 6/15 to ME 16 west to US 201 north, back to ME 6/15, which heads east and then south back to Greenville.

Start and Finish: ME 6/15 and Lily Bay Road in downtown Greenville, Maine. There are several shops and restaurants downtown worth wandering into, and you will want to walk down to the pier where

Distance
145 miles round-trip
Approximate Driving Time
3 hours 45 minutes
Peak Time
First week of October
Services
Bingham, Forks, Jackman, Greenville
Fees
None

 View of the Kennebec River valley from US 201.

The Katahdin is docked between sightseeing boat tours of Moosehead Lake.

🔘 **GPS coordinates:**
N 45 27.534, W 69 35.499.

From Greenville, follow ME 6/15 south for the 22-mile drive to ME 16 in Abbot Village. The drive is uneventful except for the miles of fall foliage lining the road. You also pass through the little town of Monson,

drive (25 miles) through forestland and one small town—Kingsbury. In Bingham, turn right on US 201, where the road seems to be one giant moose crossing, as it parallels the Kennebec River for about 20 miles of the 50-mile journey north to Jackman.

Hot Spot: Kennebec River overlook. Almost immediately after leaving Bingham, ME 16 travels north adjacent to the Kennebec River, which is wide and slow here due to a dam in Moscow. The hydroelectric dam, built in the 1930s at a cost of $7 million, was the biggest construction project ever undertaken in the state of Maine up until that time. Today, this part of the river is called Wyman Lake and there are several excellent views of the lake and hills from a trio of rest areas on the left side of the road. Our favorite is the one 9 miles north of Bingham, where a grove of paper birch trees nicely frames the view. The rest areas offer interpretive signage on the dam project, Native American use of the river, and how Benedict Arnold transported troops up the river in his ill-fated attempt to attack British forces in Quebec City during the early days of the Revolutionary War.

◉ **GPS coordinates:**
N 45 9.271, W 69 57.160.

best known as the entry point to the 100-Mile Wilderness, the remote section of the Appalachian Trail between Monson and Baxter State Park to the east. In Abbot Village, turn right on ME 16 for another long

Another 12 miles north on US 201 brings you to The Forks, the town at the center of whitewater rafting in the Kennebec Valley. The Kennebec and its tributary, the Dead

River, offer some of the best whitewater paddling opportunities in the northeastern U.S., and if you are up for the adventure, The Forks is the place to be. US 201 soon crosses the confluence of the Dead and the Kennebec, then leaves the river behind as it continues north to Jackman, about 30 miles north of The Forks.

Hot Spot: Big Wood Pond scenic overlook. Four miles south of Jackman, there is a parking area on the right, where the road is high above the valley to the west. There's not much to do here but take in the long views of forests, ponds, and mountains. However, the view is spectacular, especially if you have timed your visit with peak foliage.

◉ **GPS coordinates:**
N 45 35.062, W 70 10.954.

In Jackman, turn right on ME 6/15 for another long drive through lightly populated woods. In addition to forest, you will pass views of Long Pond and Brassua Lake be-fore running into Moosehead Lake in the little town of Rockwood.

Hot Spot: Mount Kineo view. Just over 19 miles east of Jackman, turn left on Village Road and follow it for 0.5 mile to a public boat dock in Rockwood. About a mile across the water are the 700-foot-high cliffs of Mount Kineo, the lake's most prominent landmark and a popular hiking destination (see "Mount Kineo Leg Stretcher").

◉ **GPS coordinates:**
N 45 40.610, W 69 44.363.

From the dock, continue on Village Road, which ends at ME 6/15; turn left. From here it is 19 miles back to Greenville. Like most of the trip, this stretch of 6/15 is heavily forested; moose sightings are common. The lake is tantalizingly close on the left, but there are few glimpses of it through the trees, except for where the road crosses the outlet of the lake and the beginning of the Kennebec River at a dam about 6.5 miles south of Rockwood.

🔺 Mount Kineo in Maine's Moosehead Lake.

Mount Kineo
Leg Stretcher

Mount Kineo has been a popular hiking destination for 150 years (Henry David Thoreau made two trips here in the 1850s). For several thousand years before that, the mountain's cliffs were an important source of flint for Native Americans. Stone tools and arrowheads made from Kineo flint have been found in several locations in the eastern U.S. and Canada. This hike is unusual in that it starts on a boat. To get to the trailhead, you need to park at the public boat dock in Rockwood and take the Kineo Shuttle, which leaves every other hour from 9 a.m. to 5 p.m. ($10 round-trip.) From the dock in Kineo, find the footpath that follows the southern shoreline of the island, and then hike the Indian Trail to the summit and its lookout tower. This trail is very steep and exposed, providing excellent views from several places, but if you prefer a more moderate climb, you can use the Bridle Trail instead. The hike is about 4 miles long and will take approximately three hours.

● **GPS coordinates:**
N 45 41.464, W 69 44.028.

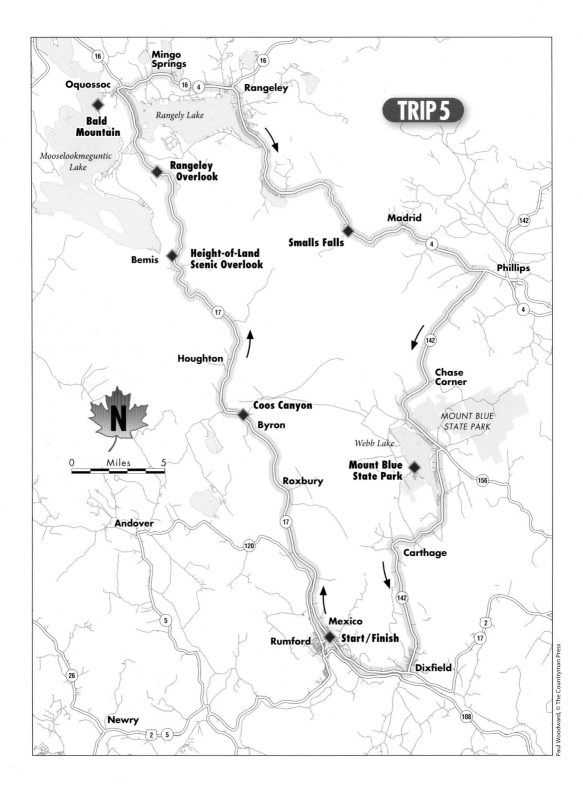

TRIP 5

16 Mingo Springs

Oquossoc

Bald Mountain

16   16 4

Rangeley

Rangely Lake

Mooselookmeguntic Lake

Rangeley Overlook

Madrid

142

Smalls Falls

Bemis

Height-of-Land Scenic Overlook

4

Phillips

17

4

Houghton

142

Chase Corner

MOUNT BLUE STATE PARK

Coos Canyon

Byron

Webb Lake

N

Mount Blue State Park

156

0   Miles   5

Roxbury

17

Andover

120

Carthage

5

142

26

17

Mexico

Start/Finish

Rumford

2

17

Dixfield

Newry

2 5

108

Paul Woodward. © The Countryman Press

Maine's Rangeley Lake Region

The Trip: This trip is a great way to spend a half day or more looking out at big views of mountainsides, lakes, and whitewater rivers awash in fall color. The towns along the way are fairly nondescript, making the wilderness experience of what is prime moose country the main reward. The big draw is Rangeley Lake and the scenic overlooks on ME 17 south of the lake, but the trip also passes by two beautiful waterfalls and through thick hardwood forests interspersed with open farmland. There are also good hiking and paddling opportuni-

Distance
95 miles round-trip
Approximate Driving Time
2 hours 30 minutes
Peak Time
Last week of September and first week of October
Services
Mexico/Rumford, Rangeley, Dixfield
Fees
None

ties around Webb Lake in Mount Blue State Park, in Weld.

Basic Route: This trip loops around a big swath of the Northern Forest, starting in Mexico, Maine, and following ME 17 north, ME 4 south, ME 142 south, and US 2 west.

Start and Finish: US 2 and ME 17 in Mexico, Maine. The twin Androscoggin River cities of Rumford and Mexico are classic Northern Forest mill towns with a decidedly blue-collar feel and plenty of restaurants and other services. Check out the river park in Rumford with its views of the falls at the Rumford Dam. To start the trip, drive north on ME 17.

◉ **GPS coordinates:**
N 44 33.417, W 70 32.589.

Hot Spot: Coos Canyon. Quickly leaving civilization behind, you reach the tiny village of Byron and Coos Canyon in 13.5 miles. There is a parking area on the right next to the dramatic little gorge, where the rushing water of the Swift River drops over

● Coos Canyon, Byron, Maine.

smoothly polished bedrock in a series of powerful waterfalls. The best view is from the bridge over the river. You can also scramble down to the water in places, but be very cautious, as the rocks can be slippery.

● **GPS coordinates:**
N 44 43.217, W 70 37.940.

Hot Spot: ME 17 Scenic Overlooks. North of Coos Canyon, ME 17 enters even wilder country, following the Swift River for several miles before climbing to the watershed between Rangeley Lake and the Androscoggin River valley. There are several viewpoints on the way up, the most notable being the Height of Land Scenic Overlook (11.5 miles north of Coos Canyon) and the Rangeley Scenic Overlook (17.5 miles north of Coos Canyon). The views of nearby mountains, Mooselookmeguntic Lake, and Rangely Lake are sweeping and beautiful.

● **GPS coordinates:**
Height of Land—N 44 50.304, W 70 42.611, Rangeley—N 44 54.392, W 70 43.581.

The views continue as ME 17 descends toward the lake, reaching ME 4 between Rangeley and Mooselookmeguntic, 5.3 miles north of the Rangeley Overlook. Turn right on ME 4. In about 7 miles, you will pass through the village of Rangeley, and its short Main Street, home to several shops, restaurants, and hotels. Just south of town is an excellent scenic view of the lake from water level, which, if it's a sunny and calm fall day, will make you wish you had a boat.

 View of Mooselookmeguntic Lake from Height of Land Scenic Overlook.

Bald Mountain
Leg Stretcher

Bald Mountain is a small peak between Rangeley and Mooselookmeguntic lakes with a fire tower and panoramic views. The hike up is relatively steep and can be wet and rough in sections, climbing 750 feet over 1 mile to the fire tower. The summit is covered in evergreens, but they quickly give way to colorful hardwoods on the lower slopes. The hike takes about an hour and 45 minutes up and back. To get to the trailhead, follow ME 4 west (left) from ME 17, and then turn left on Bald Mountain Road in about 1 mile. The trailhead is on the left in 0.9 mile.

◉ **GPS coordinates:**
N 44 57.119, W 70 47.491.

Mount Blue State Park Leg Stretcher

About 1 mile south of ME 156, West Side Road leaves ME 142 and leads right toward the campground and beach on Webb Lake in Mount Blue State Park, which can make for a nice picnic spot. There is a public boat launch near the beach, which has excellent views of nearby Mount Blue and Tumbledown Mountain. There are several good half-day and daylong hikes up the mountains, which have some spectacular views of Webb Lake and the surrounding forest. The hiking options are too numerous to mention here, but you can get more info at the park headquarters, or pick up the Appalachian Mountain Club's *Maine Mountain Guide* or Cloe Chunn's *50 Hikes in the Maine Mountains*.

◉ **GPS coordinates:**
N 44 40.962, W 70 27.042.

Hot Spot: Smalls Falls. Just over 11 miles south of the lake view in Rangeley, look for the Smalls Falls Rest Area on the right side of ME 4. Park and walk the short trail to the base of the falls, which drop 50-plus feet over four or five drops through a small gorge of beautiful multihued bedrock. You can also climb to the top of the falls via a short trail that is accessed by a small footbridge that crosses the Sandy River near the base of the falls.

◉ **GPS coordinates:**
N 44 51.534, W 70 31.006.

Continue south on ME 4 for 8.2 miles, turning right on ME 142 in Phillips. ME 142 weaves its way south through forests and farms toward Mount Blue State Park in Weld. Turn right 8.5 miles south of ME 4 to stay on ME 142. When you reach the end of ME 142 in Dixfield, turn right on US 2 for the final 5 miles of the trip, returning to ME 17 in Mexico.

PART II

Appalachian Vistas

Mount Mansfield as seen from Jeffersonville, Vermont.

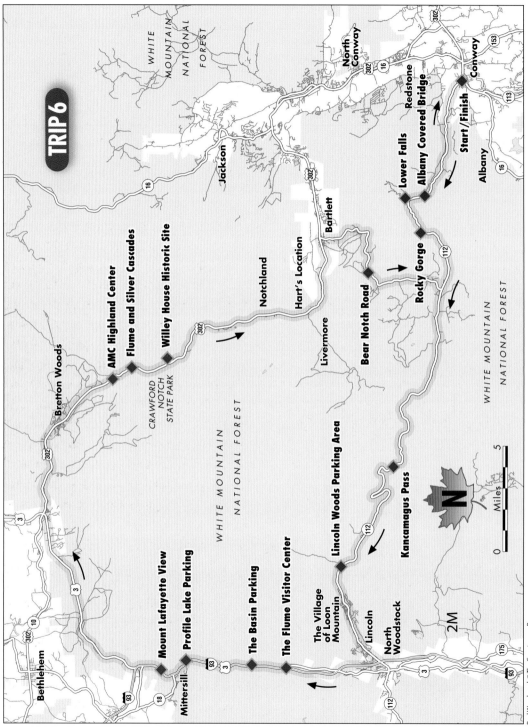

TRIP 6

WHITE MOUNTAIN NATIONAL FOREST

North Conway

Redstone

Conway

Lower Falls

Albany Covered Bridge

Start/Finish

Albany

Jackson

Bartlett

Notchland

Hart's Location

Rocky Gorge

Bear Notch Road

AMC Highland Center

Flume and Silver Cascades

Willey House Historic Site

Bretton Woods

CRAWFORD NOTCH STATE PARK

WHITE MOUNTAIN NATIONAL FOREST

Livermore

WHITE MOUNTAIN NATIONAL FOREST

Lincoln Woods Parking Area

Kancamagus Pass

N

Miles

Mount Lafayette View

Profile Lake Parking

The Basin Parking

The Flume Visitor Center

The Village of Loon Mountain

Lincoln

North Woodstock

Bethlehem

Mittersill

2M

Paul Woodward, © The Countryman Press

Classic White Mountains Tour: Crawford and Franconia Notches

Distance

110 miles round-trip

Approximate Driving Time

3 hours

Peak Time

First and second weeks of October

Services

Lincoln, Twin Mountain, and Conway (a short drive north on NH 16 from the starting point.)

Fees

A White Mountain National Forest parking pass is required to park at several of the parking areas listed in this trip description. Day passes ($3) can be purchased at the parking areas. Weeklong passes ($5) and annual passes ($20) can be purchased at the Saco Ranger Station (on NH 112 near NH 16) and at the White Mountains National Forest visitor centers in North Woodstock and Lincoln.

The Trip: This 110-mile loop visits some of the most scenic and popular parts of New Hampshire's White Mountains. From the lofty heights of the Kancamagus Highway (aka "the Kanc") and Bear Notch Road to the dramatic cliffs towering above the valley floor in Franconia and Crawford Notches, there is hardly a curve in the road that doesn't reveal a new stunning vista. Throughout the drive, you will find rushing whitewater, dramatic cliffs, mountain views, and beautiful waterfalls. The hardwood forests with the best color are on the eastern end of the Kanc, parts of US 302, and on Bear Notch Road. Higher elevations feature the bright yellows of birch trees mixed with the greens of spruce and fir trees. Although this loop can be driven in only three hours, you will probably want to devote an entire day to the excursion, as there are more than a dozen worthwhile places to pull over and take pictures or go for a walk. Most of this route is well known to leaf peepers, so expect company. Your best bet is to avoid sunny weekends when traffic on the Kancamagus Highway can be stop-and-go in the few miles around Lincoln.

Basic Route: The loop follows this basic route: from NH 16 follow NH 112 (Kancamagus Highway) west to I-93 north. Stay on I-93 north through Franconia Notch to Exit 35, US 3 north. Follow US 3 north to US 302 east (right). Stay on US 302 for 24 miles, turning right to follow Bear Notch Road back to NH 112. Turn left to return to NH 16.

Start: Kancamagus Highway (NH 112) at NH 16 in Conway, New Hampshire. There is nothing special about this starting point, but 0.1 mile west on NH 112 is the Forest Service's Saco Ranger Station, which includes a good bookstore. Start your trip by driving west on NH 112.

◉ **GPS coordinates:**
N 43 58.692, W 71 8.004.

Kancamagus Highway Hot Spots:

Albany Bridge. On the right, 6.5 miles west of NH 16, is Albany Bridge, a historic covered bridge spanning the whitewater of the Swift River. Built in 1858, this Paddleford truss–style bridge is 120 feet long and offers a pleasant view upstream of the river and distant peaks. If you feel like a walk, cross the bridge and turn left, following the dirt forest road next to the river.

◉ **GPS coordinates:**
N 44.0.335, W 71.14.497.

Lower Falls. Continuing west for another mile brings you to a parking area for Lower Falls, a wide part of the Swift River that features many cascades and one dramatic 10-foot drop. A popular swimming hole in the summer, Lower Falls is an excellent place to see some great fall color, as the river is lined with sugar maples, birches, and aspens. Across the river from the parking area, the terrain rises steeply to the Painted Cliffs, which get their name from the colored mineral stains in the rock.

◉ **GPS coordinates:**
N 44 0.935, W 71 14.727.

Rocky Gorge. In another 2.25 miles is Rocky Gorge, a small but deep gorge carved out of granite by the Swift River. A footbridge spans the river, giving a bird's-eye view of the gorge. Beyond the bridge is the Lovequist Loop, a 1-mile trail that circles Falls Pond and offers good views of the foliage around the pond and on the lower slopes of Bear Mountain.

◉ **GPS coordinates:**
N 44 0.116, W 71 16.655.

Kancamagus Pass Overlook. The road twists and turns, eventually leaving the Swift River to climb over the divide separating the Swift and Pemigewasset river watersheds. About 23 miles from NH 16 is Kancamagus Pass, the high point (2,930 feet) of the Kanc. There are overlooks on either side of the road, with views facing

🔺 View of Mount Lafayette from Governor Hugh Gallen Memorial.

east and west (great sunrise and sunset views here). Peaks covered in fall color recede to the horizon in all directions.

⬤ **GPS coordinates:**
N 44 1.695, W 71 29.778.

Lincoln Woods. Descending toward Lincoln from Kancamagus Pass, you will pass several more overlooks before the road bottoms out in the valley of the East Branch of the Pemigewasset River at Lincoln Woods. If you park at Lincoln Woods, you can walk out over "the Pemi" on a suspension bridge with great views of the fast-moving, rock-strewn river and the distant peaks of the Bond Range. Sugar maples and paper

🔺 Fall colors reflected in the Saco River, Bartlett, New Hampshire.

birches give the scene nice color. You can also take a 6.5-mile round-trip hike along the Wilderness Trail to Franconia Falls (you will need to pick up a free visitor permit from the ranger station at the trailhead before visiting the falls).

● **GPS coordinates:**
N 44 3.801, W 71 35.354.

Beyond Lincoln Woods, the Kanc soon passes Loon Mountain ski area and the hotels and strip malls of Lincoln before reaching I-93, approximately 36 miles from NH 16 and the start of the trip. To head toward Franconia Notch, take I-93 north.

● **GPS coordinates:**
N 44 2.179, W 71 40.631.

Franconia Notch Hot Spots:

The Flume. Just 4 miles after getting on I-93, exit 34A takes you to the Flume Gorge and Visitor Center in Franconia Notch State Park. The Flume is an impressive 800-foot-long gorge at the base of Mount Liberty. Only 12 to 20 feet wide, the Flume has 60- to 80-foot-high walls of granite that rise up from the West Branch of the Pemigewasset. A footbridge leads through the gorge and climbs the head of the gorge next to the beautiful Avalanche Falls. The walk is moderately strenuous and there is an entrance fee of $12.

◉ **GPS coordinates:**
N 44 5.965, W 71 40.939.

The Basin. About 2.5 miles north of the Flume on I-93 is a parking area for the Basin, a small waterfall that has carved out a smooth, circular pool at its base. If you're a fan of waterfalls, you can hike the nearby, moderately strenuous, Basin-Cascades Trail, which follows Cascade Brook, passing three waterfalls and views of the Franconia Range in its first mile.

◉ **GPS coordinates:**
N 44 7.200, W 71 40.911.

Profile Lake. Profile Lake (exit 34B) offers dramatic views of the cliffs of Cannon Mountain and the forests at the mountain's base. This was also the main viewing area for the Old Man of the Mountain, a series of stone ledges that when viewed from a certain angle resembled a craggy face in profile. Also known as the Great Stone Face, the 40-foot-tall granite outcropping, 1,200 feet above Profile Lake, was one of New Hampshire's most popular tourist attractions, and is featured on the New Hampshire state quarter. Despite attempts to shore up the outcropping, which had degraded in the face of centuries of freezing and thawing cycles, it collapsed in May 2003.

◉ **GPS coordinates:**
N 44 10.074, W 71 40.971.

Mount Lafayette View. About 1.5 miles beyond Profile Lake, take exit 34C and turn right, following the road to the left, where it will dead-end at the Governor Hugh Gallen Memorial. The memorial itself is not of much interest to leaf peepers, but you will want to venture the 100 yards or so out onto the old US 3 bridge that spans Lafayette Brook. From the bridge, there is an excellent view to the east of the fall colors at the base of Mount Lafayette as well as the rocky summit itself. The bridge is also high enough to provide western views across the Connecticut River valley to the Green Mountains of Vermont.

◉ **GPS coordinates:**
N 44 10.976, W 71 41.135.

After taking in the view, return to I-93 north and follow it for 3 miles to US 3 north (exit 35), which winds its way

through colorful forests for several miles before passing through the hamlet of Twin Mountain (several motels and one gas station); turn right here on US 302 (east), 10.5 miles north of I-93. US 302 follows the Ammonoosuc River for several miles before it curves to the south, passing several views of Mount Washington and the Presidential Range on its way to Crawford Notch.

Crawford Notch Hot Spots:

Appalachian Mountain Club's Highland Center. Just before entering Crawford Notch, you will see the AMC's Highland Center on the right. This is a beautiful mountain lodge and education center with stunning views of forests and mountains. Stop in for a meal and information about local hikes—there are several short hikes (less than an hour in length) from the center that make excellent foliage walks.

◉ **GPS coordinates:**
N 44 13.156, W 71 24.646.

Flume and Silver Cascades. About a mile south of the Highland Center on US 302, there is a parking area on the right for Flume and Silver Cascades, a pair of waterfalls that tumble in thin ribbons down the side of Mount Jackson. During peak foliage, the cascades are framed by brilliantly colored maple and birch trees.

◉ **GPS coordinates:**
N 44 12.378, W 71 24.199.

Willey House Historical Site. Two miles south of Silver Cascade is the Willey House Historical Site, which is home to Crawford Notch State Park Headquarters and a gift shop. Across the street is a short trail around Willey Pond, which has excellent views of the mountains that form Crawford Notch.

◉ **GPS coordinates:**
N 44 10.924, W 71 23.92.

Continuing south through the notch on US 302, you will find several pull-offs with more views of the mountains, as well as the Saco River, which parallels the road for several miles. When you reach the village of Bartlett, keep an eye out for Bear Notch Road on the right, which is 15 miles south of the Highland Center. Turn right on Bear Notch Road (closed in winter) for a twisty drive up to the pass that divides the Crawford Notch area from the Kancamagus region. Several pull-offs provide excellent long views of the valley below and the distant Presidential Range. Bear Notch Road ends at the Kancamagus Highway, 9 miles from US 302. Turn left here to make the 20-minute drive back to your starting point at NH 16.

◀ Silver Cascades, Crawford Notch State Park.

White Mountains, near Crawford Notch State Park.

White Mountain Leg Stretchers

There are literally dozens of walks and hikes that can be started from various points on this tour, from all-day epic affairs to short 20-minute walks. If hiking is your thing, check out *50 Hikes in the White Mountains* by Daniel Doan or our own *Discover the White Mountains*. You can also get expert opinions on hikes in the area from the rangers at the Saco Ranger Station in Conway and from the staff at the AMC's Highland Center in Crawford Notch. Here are three of our favorite shorter hikes.

Boulder Loop Trail. This hike starts near the Albany Covered Bridge and climbs about 900 feet to ledges overlooking the Swift River valley and the Sandwich Range. The 3-mile round-trip hike takes about two hours.

Bald Mountain and Artists Bluff. This 1.5-mile hike provides stunning views of the Franconia Range, for minimal effort. The trailhead is on NH 18 at the northern entrance to Franconia Notch.

Mount Willard. Starting from the Highland Center, the Mount Willard Trail climbs 900 feet over 1.6 miles to the ledges at the top of the cliffs on Mount Willard. The views of Crawford Notch are spectacular. Give yourself about two hours to complete this hike.

Vermont's Smugglers' Notch

The Trip: This short drive between Stowe and Jeffersonville, Vermont, is one of the most scenic drives in the state as it connects two classic New England villages by climbing up and over one of the more dramatic notches in the Green Mountains. Stowe is a busy ski town that maintains its rural charm with white steepled churches and thousands of acres of farmland. Jeffersonville is a sleepy hamlet with only a couple of restaurants, a pair of art galleries, and one gas station, but the views of Mount Mansfield from the nearby cornfields are worth the drive down from the notch. The real attraction here, though, is

Distance
18 miles one-way
Approximate Driving Time
30 minutes
Peak Time
First and second weeks of October
Services
Stowe, Jeffersonville
Fees
None

Smugglers' Notch, where the road narrows to one lane, reaches 2,162 feet of elevation, and is walled in by cliffs that are as high as 1,000 feet. And yes, the notch is reputed to have been used by smugglers (cattle and liquor) in the past. The foliage in the notch is limited to the yellows of birches and the greens of conifers, but there are the traditional reds and oranges of a New England fall in the valley portions of this trip.

Basic Route: This trip follows VT 108 for its entirety. It starts from VT 100 in Stowe and ends in Jeffersonville, 18 miles away.

Start: **VT 108 at VT 100** in Stowe, Vermont. Along Stowe's Main Street (VT 100), there are numerous shops, galleries, and restaurants to explore. Begin this drive by heading west on VT 108.

◉ **GPS coordinates:**
N 44 27.927, W 72 41.245.

At its start VT 108 plies through a string of motels and strip malls, occasionally interrupted by mountain views and the rushing waters of the West Branch of the Little River (a 5.3-mile recreation path starts in

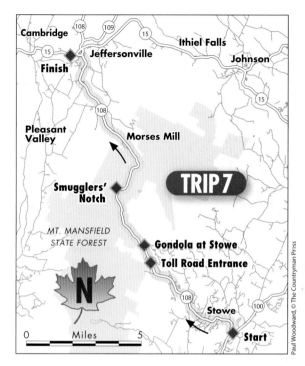

town and follows the river for parts of its length). Six miles from downtown, you will pass the historic Auto Toll Road on the left ($24 fee), which leads 7 miles to the Mount Mansfield Summit Station. This is a great diversion if you want to see the Green Mountains from Vermont's highest peak (the road closes after Columbus Day). Another 6.5 miles brings you to the gondola at Stowe ski area (around $20 round-trip—visit www.stowe.com for current rates), which is another way to access Mount Mansfield.

Hot Spot: Smugglers' Cave. After passing the ski area, VT 108 becomes a narrow and

VT 108 in Smugglers' Notch.

Sterling Pond Leg Stretcher

Across VT 108 from Smugglers' Cave, the Long Trail climbs 800 feet in 1.2 miles to Sterling Pond, a small pond on the northwestern slope of Spruce Peak. The hike is strenuous and takes about three hours round-trip, but has excellent rewards at the end: solitude on the wooded shores of the pond and views of the peaks and valleys to the west and north. Stay on the Long Trail (look for the white trail blazes on the trees marking the trail) all the way to Sterling Pond and Sterling Pond Shelter. If you like fly-fishing, bring your gear—at 3,008 feet above sea level, this is the highest trout pond in Vermont. For more info about this hike and others in the Green Mountains, check out *50 Hikes in Vermont* (The Countryman Press) or the Green Mountain Club's *Long Trail Guide*.

curvy mountain road, offering several parking areas where you can pull off and explore the natural landscape. At the top of the notch is Smugglers' Cave, featuring a huge boulder field comprised of giant rocks that have fallen from the cliffs above. A trail leads from the parking area to climb up through the boulders on the west side of the road. A few minutes' walk brings you to nice views of the notch and the valley to the north.

◉ **GPS coordinates:**
N 44 33.373, W 72 47.681.

Beyond Smugglers' Cave, northern-facing vistas open up as VT 108 begins its descent to Jeffersonville. As the road bottoms out, you will pass through typical Vermont farmland before reaching Jeffersonville, 18 miles from VT 100.

Finish: VT108 and VT 15 in Jeffersonville.

◉ **GPS coordinates:**
N 44 38.622, W 72 49.759.

Vermont Route 100 Mountain Gaps

The Trip: This trip in the Green Mountains of central Vermont offers the classic New England vista: red barns in fields surrounded by hillsides ablaze in autumn color. While the entire length of VT 100 has much to offer, the middle portion of the highway offers access to two of the more scenic mountain-gap roads in the state—VT 125 and Lincoln Gap. You will probably want to devote half a day to this trip, stopping to check out waterfalls, the views from the gap roads, and the shops and restaurants in Bristol. Foliage seems to peak a little earlier along VT 100 than it does on the western slopes of the Green Mountains, which you will see while driving VT 116. If you visit during the first two weeks of October you are almost guaranteed to see peak color on at least some portions of this route.

Basic Route: This trip starts at the intersection of VT 100 and VT 125 in Hancock and heads west on VT 125. It follows VT 125 up and through Middlebury Gap to VT 116 in East Middlebury. Turn right here and follow VT 116 north to Bristol; turn right here onto VT 17, following it through town to Lincoln Road in 2.6 miles. Turn right here for the drive through Lincoln Gap (closed in winter), and then the final 14.5 miles on VT 100 south to the start of the loop at VT 125.

Start: **VT 125 at VT 100** in Hancock, Vermont. There's not much here but a general store, so pick up some cheese or doughnuts and coffee and start your trip by heading west on VT 125.

◉ **GPS coordinates:**
N 43 55.576, W 72 50.502.

Distance	
56 miles round-trip	
Approximate Driving Time	
1 hour 40 minutes	
Peak Time	
First and second weeks of October	
Services	
Bristol	
Fees	
None	

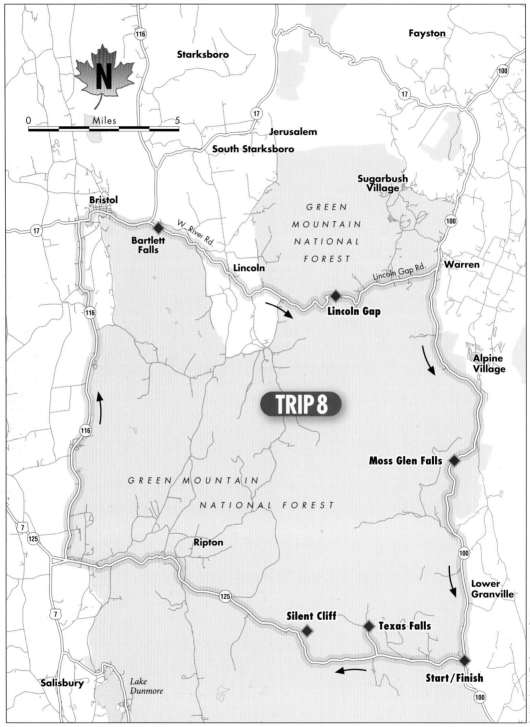

116

Starksboro

Fayston

N

100

0   Miles   5

17

Jerusalem

South Starksboro

17

Sugarbush
Village

Bristol

GREEN

MOUNTAIN

100

W. River Rd.

Bartlett
Falls

NATIONAL

17

Lincoln

FOREST

Lincoln Gap Rd.

Warren

116

Lincoln Gap

Alpine
Village

TRIP 8

Moss Glen Falls

116

GREEN MOUNTAIN

NATIONAL FOREST

100

7

125

Ripton

Lower
Granville

125

7

Silent Cliff

Texas Falls

Start/Finish

Salisbury

Lake
Dunmore

100

Paul Woodward, © The Countryman Press

Hot Spot: Texas Falls. In only 3 miles, you will encounter your first diversion: turn right toward the Texas Falls Recreation Area in the Green Mountain National Forest. A mile of quiet gravel road brings you to the parking area for the falls, on the right side. This is where the Hancock Branch of the White River squeezes through a narrow cleft of beautifully sculpted bedrock. A 1.2-mile nature trail explores the woods across the river and makes for a nice walk on a cool autumn day with peak colors.

◉ **GPS coordinates:**
N 43 56.142, W 72 54.076.

After visiting the falls, head back to VT 125 and continue west, climbing up to Middlebury Gap, which has good views to the

▼ Barn on VT 100 in Hancock, Vermont.

🔺 Mount Abraham as seen from Lincoln, Vermont.

on VT 116. The road meanders through rural Vermont with views of the Green Mountains on the right for 10 miles before reaching the town of Bristol. In Bristol, turn right on VT 17, where the road becomes a wide avenue bordered by numerous shops and restaurants.

After Bristol, VT 17 reaches Lincoln Road in 2.6 miles after crossing the New Haven River. Turn right here for the drive up to Lincoln Gap.

Hot Spot: Bartlett Falls. Just 0.2 miles from VT 17 is a pull-off on the right side of the road, where you can park and walk about 30 yards to a view of Bartlett Falls. Here the river is wide and drops about 15 feet into a deep pool that is popular with swimmers in warmer weather. Beyond the falls, the road parallels the river for much of the next 4 miles before it begins its climb up to Lincoln Gap.

⦿ **GPS coordinates:**
N 44 7.639, W 73 2.784.

As the road winds its way through the village of Lincoln, stay right on River Road and then continue straight on Lincoln Gap Road where South Lincoln Road leads right. Enjoy the views of Mount Abraham along the way.

Hot Spot: Lincoln Gap. Just before reaching Lincoln Gap (about 8 miles from VT 17) there are spectacular views to the south. In Lincoln Gap there is a parking area and

west as you crest the high point of the gap. The road descends the western slope of the Green Mountains and then passes through the scenic Bread Loaf campus of Middlebury College before reaching the valley floor in East Middlebury; turn right here

trailhead for the Long Trail, which hikers can take north for a 3.5-mile strenuous hike up Mount Abraham, which, at 4,006 feet above sea level, is the fifth-highest peak in Vermont. An easier hike is Sunset Ledge, 1.1 miles south on the Long Trail.

● **GPS coordinates:**

N 44 5.704, W 72 55.724.

After Lincoln Gap, the road makes a very steep 4-mile descent to VT 100 (not recommended for vehicles with trailers in tow). Turn right here for the 14.5-mile drive back to the trip start at VT 125. The drive passes beautiful farms with views of the Green Mountains and the narrow passage through the Granville Reservation State Park.

Hot Spot: Moss Glen Falls. In the heart of the Granville Reservation is Moss Glen Falls, considered by many to be the most photogenic waterfall in the state. A classic bridal-veil falls that cascades about 30 feet over dark schist, the falls are especially beautiful on a misty fall day after a good rain.

● **GPS coordinates:**

N 44 1.121, W 72 50.972.

Mountain Gap Leg Stretchers

Silent Cliff is a small ledge with some obstructed but excellent views of Middlebury Gap, the Champlain Valley, and the Adirondack Mountains in New York. From the parking area at the height of land in Middlebury Gap on VT 125, follow the white blazes of the Long Trail north for a steep 0.4-mile climb to the Silent Cliff Trail (blue blazes), where you should turn right for an easier 0.4-mile climb to the cliff. The 1.6-mile up-and-back trip takes about an hour.

Eastwood's Rise and Sunset Ledge are a pair of overlooks on the Long Trail south of Lincoln Gap. Both provide excellent views west over western Vermont to the Adirondacks. From the parking area at the top of the gap, follow the white blazes of the Long Trail south for 0.4 mile to Eastwood's Rise and then another 0.7 mile to Sunset Ledge. Wear sturdy footwear, as the trail is rocky, sometimes muddy, and gains about 400 feet of elevation. The up-and-back trip to Sunset Ledge should take about an hour.

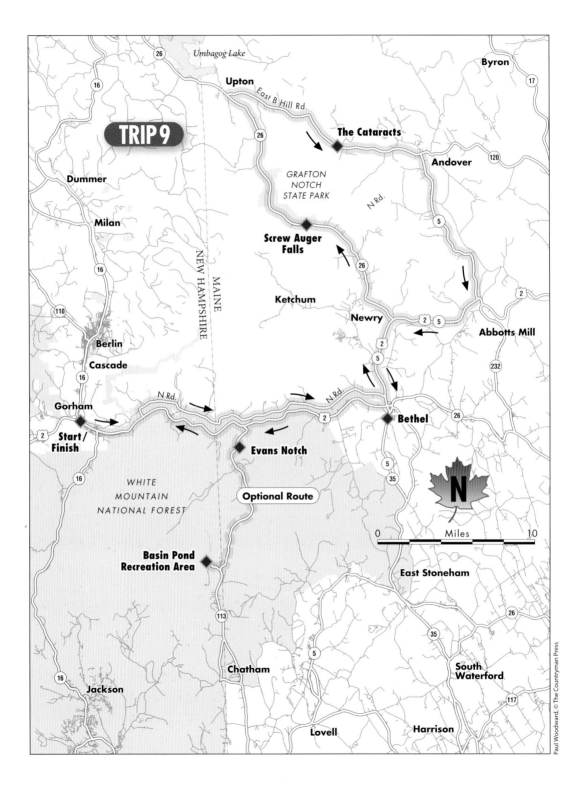

Umbagog Lake

Byron

Upton

East B Hill Rd.

The Cataracts

Andover

GRAFTON
NOTCH
STATE PARK

Dummer

N Rd.

Milan

Screw Auger
Falls

Ketchum

Newry

Abbotts Mill

NEW HAMPSHIRE

MAINE

Berlin

Cascade

N Rd.

N Rd.

Gorham

Bethel

Start /
Finish

Evans Notch

WHITE
MOUNTAIN
NATIONAL FOREST

Optional Route

N

Basin Pond
Recreation Area

East Stoneham

0   Miles   10

Chatham

South
Waterford

Jackson

Lovell

Harrison

TRIP 9

Paul Woodward, © The Countryman Press

Maine's Grafton Notch

The Trip: The rugged beauty of northern New England is at its best in Maine's Grafton Notch State Park, where ME 26 squeezes between high peaks and the Bear River tumbles over smoothly sculptured granite potholes. This trip explores the length of the notch, but also meanders through pastoral scenery and remote northern forests. It starts in Gorham, New Hampshire, the northern gateway to the White Mountains, and then passes through Bethel, Maine, a charming ski village near the Sunday River ski area. The other towns on this loop are small and spread out, and

usually offer just a general store and gas station, so for much of the trip you will experience the remoteness of Maine's North Woods. At peak foliage time, usually the first week of October, there is good color along most of the route. Plan to spend at least half a day making this trip.

Basic Route: This trip starts at the intersection of NH 16 and US 2 in Gorham, following US 2 east for a short distance before crossing the Androscoggin River on North Road, which then parallels the river most of the way to ME 26 in Bethel, Maine. Following ME 26, the trip then heads through Grafton Notch. North of the notch, turn right on the mostly gravel East B Hill Road, which meanders through thick forests for 14 miles to US 5 in Andover, Maine. From here, take US 5 to US 2 in Bethel, then follow US 2 west back to the start of the trip in Gorham.

Start: NH 16 and US 2 in Gorham, New Hampshire. Gorham is a blue-collar former paper-mill town that is making the transi-

Distance	
105 miles round-trip	
Approximate Driving Time	
1 hour 45 minutes	
Peak Time	
First week of October	
Services	
Gorham, Bethel	
Fees	
None	

🔺 Screw Auger Falls, Grafton Notch State Park.

tion to a tourist economy. If you need to stock up on gas and provisions or grab a cup of coffee (try the White Mountain Café), head west into Gorham on US 2 for about 0.5 mile before starting the trip by heading east on US 2.

◉ **GPS coordinates:**
N 44 23.542, W 71 11.15.

About 3 miles east of Gorham, turn left on North Road, crossing the Androscoggin River before bearing right. North Road meanders in the river valley, through forests and farmland with views of the Moriah Range, before ending at US 2/US 5/ME 26 about 16 miles later in Bethel. To head into town, turn right, but to make the drive to Grafton Notch, turn left and head north. In 5 miles, follow ME 26 to the left where it leaves US 2 and US 5, heading north past small farms and big vistas in Newry on its way to Grafton Notch State Park.

Hot Spot: Screw Auger Falls. As you enter the state park, the valley gets narrower and the peaks taller, with the Mahoosuc Range on the left and the Baldpate Range on the right (both top out at over 4,000 feet). Ten miles after leaving US 2, there will be a parking area on the left for Screw Auger Falls. While there are several other small falls in the area, Screw Auger is the most impressive, as the Bear River falls in several cascades over smoothly polished granite before plunging 45 feet over a series of six falls.

◉ **GPS coordinates:**
N 44 34.311, W 70 54.158.

Beyond the notch, the landscape flattens out as it nears the town of Upton; turn right here on East B Hill Road, also called

Andover Road. This gravel road is remote and for a while you will definitely feel like you are heading nowhere (don't worry, you're not lost), but there are beautiful hardwood forests along stretches of the road as well as occasional big views to the north. Fourteen miles from ME 26, you will reach the small town of Andover; turn right on US 5.

Hot Spot: The Cataracts. These falls are little visited, getting the occasional foot traffic from hikers on the Appalachian Trail, but they are worth the 200 yards of re-

🔻 Grafton Notch, from a Baldpate Range viewpoint.

quired trail walking. The Cataracts is a series of small cascades that drop a total of 60 feet over several hundred yards. After a dry spell they can be a bit disappointing, but after a good October rain, they are quite beautiful. To reach the falls, look for Appalachian Trail parking on East B Hill

🔺 ME 26 in Grafton Notch State Park.

Optional Side Trip: Evans Notch

Evans Notch is an outlier of the White Mountain National Forest that is little known to most visitors to the region, yet is home to some very dramatic scenery. If you find you have more time to explore as you head back to Gorham on US 2, consider making the excursion into the notch on ME 113. About 10 miles west of Bethel, ME 113 leads south along the Wild River, cruising through stands of paper birch trees and providing excellent views of the river and the Carter-Moriah Range. About 9 miles south of US 2 is the Cold River overlook, which has picnic tables and a great view to the west. In another 2 miles, the Basin Recreation Area is on the right. Turn here and follow the road to Basin Pond, offering stunning fall foliage in the bowl-shaped lower slopes of Mount Meader.

⦿ **GPS coordinates:**
N 44 16.189, W 71 1.260.

Road, about 5.5 miles east of ME 26. Follow the AT south for about 100 yards, then turn left, following the Cascade Trail for another 100 yards to the falls.

⦿ **GPS coordinates:**
N 44 40.042, W 70 53.571.

From Andover, follow US 5 south, where it passes more classic rural Maine scenery, eventually rejoining US 2 and ME 116 north of Bethel. About 22 miles south of Andover, head east on US 2 and drive the final 21 miles of the trip back to Gorham.

Massachusetts's High Point: Mount Greylock

The Trip: This trip loops around the northern half of Berkshire County, which is known for its mountain summits, narrow river valleys, bustling mill towns, and college greens. By October, the summer arts festivals the area is famous for have ended, but the scenery is at its best in the fall as the northern hardwood forests of the mountains reach their peaks and the river forests of oak and hickory gleam like gold and brass in the sun. The trip starts in the region's biggest city, Pittsfield, and quickly climbs an auto road to the 360-degree views of Mount Greylock before heading back down to the towns of North Adams and Williamstown. It then jogs south through the valley separating New York's Taconic Range from the Berkshires before passing the Hancock Shaker Village and returning to Pittsfield.

Basic Route: This trip starts at the intersection of US 20 and US 7 in Pittsfield, heading north to North Main Street and then following the road to the summit of Mount Greylock. It is then a 9-mile drive down from the summit on Notch Road to MA 2 in North Adams. Follow MA 2 west to US 7 in Williamstown, then head south on US 7 to MA 43; take MA 43 south to NY 22. Following NY 22 south for 6 miles brings you back to US 20 west and the drive back to the start of the loop.

Start: US 20 and US 7 in Pittsfield, Massachusetts. Start by driving north through the center of Pittsfield, taking care to stay on US 7 north as you pass through the traffic circle and intersections in the center of town (you'll need to bear right, then take a left).

Distance
63 miles round-trip
Approximate Driving Time
1 hour 25 minutes
Peak Time
Second week of October
Services
Pittsfield, North Adams, Williamstown
Fees
$2 to park on the summit of Mount Greylock

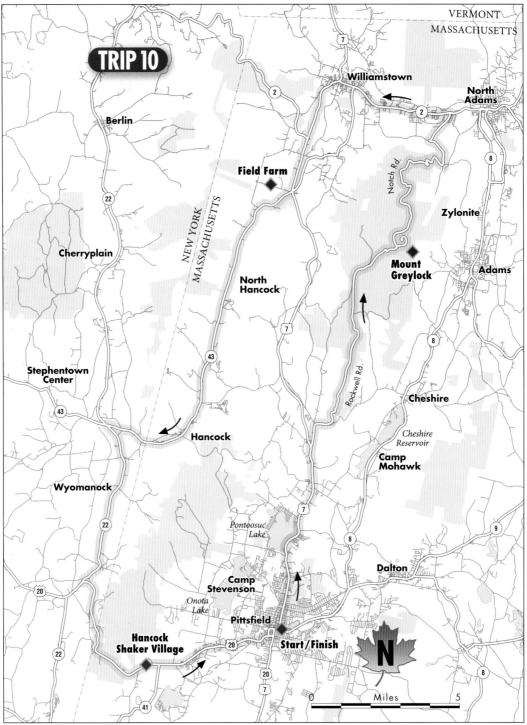

TRIP 10

VERMONT
MASSACHUSETTS

Williamstown

North
Adams

Berlin

Field Farm

Zylonite

Cherryplain

Mount
Greylock

Adams

North
Hancock

Stephentown
Center

Cheshire

Hancock

Cheshire
Reservoir

Camp
Mohawk

Wyomanock

Pontoosuc
Lake

Dalton

Camp
Stevenson

Onota
Lake

Pittsfield

N

Hancock
Shaker Village

Start/Finish

NEW YORK
MASSACHUSETTS

Notch Rd.

Rockwell Rd.

0   Miles   5

Paul Woodward. © The Countryman Press

🔺 View from a hay field, Williamstown, Massachusetts.

● **GPS coordinates:**
N 42 26.715, W 73 15.247.

After passing through Pittsfield, turn right on North Main Street, 7.1 miles north of US 20. In 0.7 mile, turn right on Quarry Road and follow the signs for the summit of Mount Greylock as you enter Mount Greylock State Reservation. The road winds its way for 10 miles through beautiful forests and past several viewpoints before reaching the summit parking area.

Hot Spot: Mount Greylock Summit. The views from the highest point in Massachusetts are spectacular, and if you are lucky to be there on a clear October day, you will be treated to a landscape rich in fall color

Money Brook Falls, Mount Greylock State Reservation.

that extends from the Berkshires to Vermont's Green Mountains. Next to the parking area is Bascom Lodge, a rustic stone and wood building constructed in the 1930s by the Civilian Conservation Corps; it still provides lodging and meals (for reservations call 917-680-0079). Numerous hiking trails leave from the summit, and you can pick up a trail map at the visitor center at the base of the auto road.

◉ **GPS coordinates:**
N 42 38.231, W 73 10.017.

From the summit, drive back down the auto road for about a mile and turn right on Notch Road, which descends the north side of the mountain, providing similar scenery as the drive up. In 7 miles, make a sharp right (Mount Williams Reservoir is straight ahead) and drive another 1.2 miles to MA 2 in North Adams. Drive west on MA 2 through the center of busy North Adams, a gritty mill town that now boasts one of the premier art museums in the state—the Massachusetts Museum of Contemporary Art. About 4 miles beyond North Adams, you will pass through the neatly manicured town of Williamstown, home to Williams College and a pair of excellent art museums—the Clark Art Institute and the Williams College Museum of Art. When you reach the traffic circle west of campus, follow US 7 south (left) for 4.5 miles to MA 43; turn right. Both US 7 and MA 43 pass through rural Berkshire

County farmland with pleasant views of orchards and hay bales against a mountain backdrop.

The rural character of the drive continues as you reach NY 22 (turn left) on the easternmost edge of New York State. Six miles later, turn left on US 20 for the final 20 miles of the drive.

Hot Spot: Hancock Shaker Village. On US 20 about 5 miles west of Pittsfield sits the Hancock Shaker Village ($15 entrance fee; www.hancockshakervillage.org). Settled in 1793, the village was the third of nineteen Shaker villages to be established in the U.S. during the 18th and 19th centuries. The village was closed by the Shaker ministry in 1960, and it opened as a museum in 1961. With 1,000 acres of farmland and forests, and 20 buildings preserved and restored, it is an excellent way to learn about 19th-century life in an American utopian village. Guided and self-guided tours are available and there is also a restaurant and children's discovery room on site.

⦿ **GPS coordinates:**
N 42 25.821, W 73 20.585.

Optional Side Trip: Field Farm

Field Farm is a 316-acre tract of fields, streams, and forests owned and managed by the Massachusetts Trustees of Reservations. Near the intersection of US 7 and MA 43 in Williamstown, this preserve makes a great place to take a break from driving and enjoy the autumn scenery on foot. Four miles of trails explore meadows, pine and hardwood forests, freshwater marshes, two streams, and a spring-fed pond. Of particular interest is the Caves Lot, where forest streams disappear underground, carving their way through the limestone to create caves and below-ground channels. There is also a sculpture garden and The Folly, a guest house that is run by the Trustees as a bed & breakfast. (For reservations, and more information about Field Farm, visit www.thetrustees.org.) To get to Field Farm, turn right on Sloan Road, just as you turn onto MA 43 from US 7. Parking is on the right in 0.5 mile.

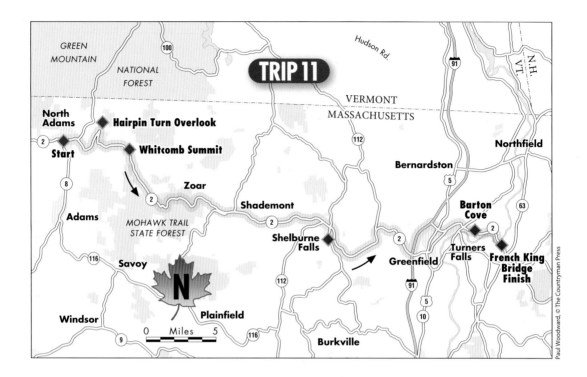

GREEN
MOUNTAIN

NATIONAL
FOREST

100

Hudson Rd.

TRIP 11

91

N.H.
VT.

VERMONT
MASSACHUSETTS

112

Northfield

North
Adams

◆ Hairpin Turn Overlook

Bernardston

2

Start

◆ Whitcomb Summit

5

8

Zoar

2

63

Shademont

Barton
Cove

2

Adams

MOHAWK TRAIL
STATE FOREST

2

Shelburne
Falls

2

Turners
Falls

116

Savoy

N

Greenfield

French King
Bridge
Finish

91

112

5

Windsor

Plainfield

10

9

0   Miles   5

116

Burkville

Paul Woodward, © The Countryman Press

The Mohawk Trail:
Historic Massachusetts Highway

The Trip: Massachusetts Route 2, better known as the Mohawk Trail, is a classic New England scenic drive that winds through narrow river valleys and climbs hairpin turns to high points in the northern Berkshires. Officially, the Mohawk Trail starts at I-495 and twists and turns for nearly 100 miles west to North Adams, though the good scenery doesn't really start until you get past the cities of Leominster, Fitchburg, and Gardner. For this trip, we have chosen to describe the western half of the road, starting in North Adams and ending at the French King Bridge over the Connecticut River in Erv-

ing. Along the way, there are big views from several high points in Florida, and intimate excursions beside the Cold and Deerfield rivers. There is also a side trip into Shelburne Falls, the "hub" of the Mohawk Trail, with its eclectic mix of restaurants, gift shops, and art galleries.

Basic Route: This trip starts on MA 2 at its intersection with MA 8 in North Adams, and follows MA 2 east for about 45 miles to the French King Bridge in Erving. At the 26-mile mark, Shelburne Falls is a 0.6-mile side trip to the right on Main Street. There is also a 3-mile segment where MA 2 coincides with I-91 north.

Start: MA 2 and MA 8 in North Adams, Massachusetts. If you have time to kill in North Adams, consider heading to the Massachusetts Museum of Contemporary Art (www.massmoca.org), about 0.25 mile north of this intersection at 87 Marshall Street.

◉ **GPS coordinates:**
N 42 42.021, W 73 6.826.

Distance
45 miles one-way
Approximate Driving Time
1 hour 15 minutes
Peak Time
First and second weeks of October
Services
North Adams, Shelburne Falls, Greenfield
Fees
None

Hot Spot: Hairpin Turn. Just 5 miles east of MA 8, the Mohawk Trail makes a sharp hairpin turn to the right. There is parking on the right side of the road, and excellent views to the north on the left. Farms, forests, small villages, and hillsides stretch all the way to Vermont.

⦿ **GPS coordinates:**
N 42 42.526, W 73 3.788.

Hot Spot: Florida Overlooks. Florida—Massachusetts, that is—has several views of the surrounding Berkshire Mountains from several viewpoints in the Hoosac Range, most notably the Western Summit, Whitcomb Summit, and the Eastern Summit. Our favorite is Whitcomb, where there are excellent views north and east over the Deerfield River valley.

⦿ **GPS coordinates:**
N 42 41.280, W 73 1.218.

After the Mohawk Trail descends the eastern slopes of the Hoosac Range, it bottoms out and parallels the Cold River for about 4 miles, winding through the narrow, heavily forested valley. The landscape opens up a bit as the Cold River empties into the Deerfield River, which the road then follows all the way to Shelburne Falls; turn right here on Main Street, 26.5 miles east of North Adams.

◁ View from hairpin turn on the Mohawk Trail, North Adams, Massachusetts.

Barton Cove
Leg Stretcher

🔺 The Connecticut River as seen from French King Bridge, Erving, Massachusetts.

About 2 miles before the French King Bridge is the Barton Cove Recreation and Camping Area (call 413-859-2960). Canoe and kayak rentals are available if you want to explore the quiet water of this section of the Connecticut River. Bald eagles nest here in the spring and early summer, and they can linger here throughout the fall and winter. There is also a great mile-long nature trail that follows the rocky shoreline of the peninsula that juts into the river on the upstream side of the cove. The trail is a great place to take in the view of fall foliage along the river. You might also want to check out the emu ranch next to the state boat launch just west of the nature area.

◉ **GPS coordinates:**
N 42 36.452, W 72 31.972.

Hot Spot: Shelburne Falls. Half a mile down Main Street is Shelburne Falls, a good place to stop for window-shopping and to grab a cup of coffee. You should also check out the view of the river from the bridge on Main Street, and walk down to the intriguing glacial potholes that pock the bedrock on the river ledges below the dam in the center of town.

◉ **GPS coordinates:**
N 42 36.196, W 72 44.387.

From Shelburne Falls, head back to MA 2 and continue east to Greenfield, where MA 2 joins I-91 north for 3 miles. Exit I-91 to stay on MA 2 east, and follow it past Turners Falls and a drive that follows the Connecticut River for 5.5 miles to the French King Bridge and the end of the trip.

Hot Spot: French King Bridge. The pedestrian walkway on the French King Bridge in Erving provides a commanding view of the Connecticut River 140 feet below the bridge deck. The bridge is named after French King Rock, the large boulder just upstream. How the rock got its name is unknown, but popular conjecture has it that it was named by the French officer of a Native American scouting party during the French and Indian War. In addition to the views from the bridge, you can get a nice view of the bridge itself, by driving over the bridge and making the first right onto River Road and following it to the confluence of the Millers and Connecticut rivers in a few hundred yards.

◉ **GPS coordinates:**
N 42 35.886, W 72 29.845.

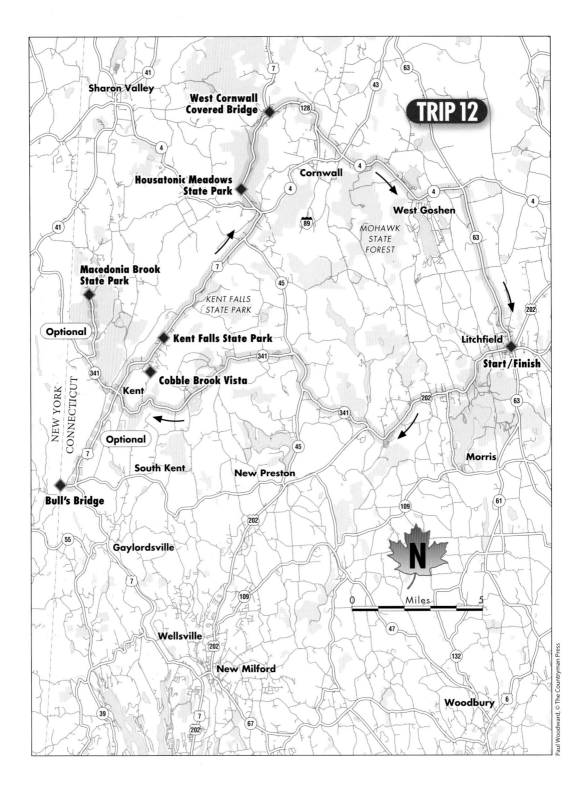

Sharon Valley

West Cornwall
Covered Bridge

TRIP 12

Cornwall

West Goshen

MOHAWK
STATE
FOREST

Housatonic Meadows
State Park

Macedonia Brook
State Park

Optional

KENT FALLS
STATE PARK

Kent Falls State Park

Cobble Brook Vista

Kent

Litchfield

Start/Finish

Optional

NEW YORK
CONNECTICUT

Morris

South Kent

New Preston

Bull's Bridge

Gaylordsville

N

0   Miles   5

Wellsville

New Milford

Woodbury

Paul Woodward, © The Countryman Press

Western Connecticut Highlands: The Litchfield Hills

The Trip: This trip in the northwest corner of Connecticut seems a world away from the industrial cities and bedroom communities found in much of the state. Its rolling hills, farms, and historic towns have more of a northern New England look and feel. While the hills aren't as lofty as the White or Green mountains, they are packed close together, creating a rugged topography that is traversed by the Appalachian Trail and drained by numerous whitewater streams that swell the Housatonic River from the Massachusetts border south to Long Island Sound. The forests here are dominated by oaks, hickories, and other hardwoods, creating a fall foliage display that is more golden and russet than the orange and red displays found farther north. While this trip uses the major scenic roads in the area, you could easily explore any number of back roads here and get pleasantly lost in rural countryside. Plan to spend a good three hours to fully enjoy this drive.

Basic Route: This trip starts and ends in Litchfield, following US 202 south to CT 341 west to Kent. From Kent, follow the Housatonic River north on US 7 to West Cornwall, then CT 128 and CT 4 east to Goshen. From Goshen, take CT 63 south back to Litchfield.

Start: US 202 and CT 63 in Litchfield, Connecticut. Litchfield is one of those scenic New England towns that draw visitors to the region. Its large town green is lined with inviting shops and restaurants, historic homes, and a beautiful white steepled Congregational church. You will want to give yourself time to walk the streets on either side of the green as well as North and

Distance
50 miles round-trip
Approximate Driving Time
1 hour 15 minutes
Peak Time
Second and third weeks of October
Services
Litchfield, Kent
Fees
$10 entrance fee to Kent Falls State Park (weekends and holidays only; free on weekdays)

Optional Side Trip: Kent

There is a lot to explore beyond Main Street in Kent. Just 4 miles south of town is **Bull's Bridge**, a covered bridge perched above an impressive set of whitewater rapids.

◉ **GPS coordinates:**
N 41 40.549 W 73 30.555.

About 1.5 miles west of town on CT 341, turn right on Macedonia Brook Road, which winds its way next to rushing streams and past stone walls in the forest of **Macedonia Brook State Park**. The park also boasts several excellent hiking trails to nice views of the Housatonic Valley.

◉ **GPS coordinates:**
N41 45.350, W 73 29.516.

Cobble Brook Vista, managed by the Weantinoge Heritage Land Trust, is another great spot to go for a short hike. About 2 miles north of CT 341, turn right on Studio Hill Road, then right again on Studio Hill Circle. A parking area will be on the right. Hike the 2.5-mile Red Loop up to a rocky ledge with views of the Housatonic.

◉ **GPS coordinates:**
N 41 44.320, W 73 27.208.

◀ Sunset at Cobble Brook Vista, Kent, Connecticut.

South Streets, which are graced with impressive mansions. The nearby White Memorial Foundation, with its 4,000 acres of forests and ponds, is also a great place to explore on foot. To begin the drive, head west on US 202.

◉ GPS coordinates:
N 41 44.838, W 73 11.404.

It takes a few miles of driving on US 202 to leave the busy world of central Connecticut behind, but by the time you reach CT 341 in 7.3 miles, you will be deep into the rural landscapes of the Litchfield Hills. Turn right on CT 341 for a 12-mile drive through beautiful hardwood forests and past farms and stone walls to US 7 in Kent. Kent, with its vibrant arts community, is another place worth spending some time. This stretch of US 7 is lined with some great shops and galleries.

Hot Spot: Kent Falls State Park. Just over 5 miles north of CT 341, Kent Falls State Park will be on your right. A small park, it is home to Kent Falls, which tumbles 70 feet over bedrock and in fall is framed by beautiful fall foliage.

◉ GPS coordinates:
N 41 46.602, W 73 25.06.

Hot Spot: Housatonic Meadows State Park. Just over 4 miles north of Kent Falls, US 7 crosses the Housatonic River, then bears right to follow the river through Housatonic Meadows State Park. There are a pair of picnic areas and a campground next to the river that make a great place to take in the fall colors and the sounds of whitewater. This stretch of the river is popular with both paddlers and fly-fishing enthusiasts.

◉ GPS coordinates:
N 41 49.528, W 73 22.763.

Hot Spot: West Cornwall Covered Bridge. A few miles north of the state park, turn right onto CT 128 and cross the river on a beautiful red covered bridge. You then arrive in West Cornwall, with its general store and old train depot, but you will most likely be inspired to stop and get your camera out to shoot the little town center, the bridge, and the river.

◉ GPS coordinates:
N 41 52.300, W 73 21.826.

To finish the trip, continue east on CT 128 for 4 miles, and then straight on US 4 east. About 5 miles later, in the little village of Goshen, turn right on CT 63 for the final 6.3 miles back to Litchfield.

▼ The Connecticut River as seen from Mount Sugarloaf in Deerfield, Massachusetts.

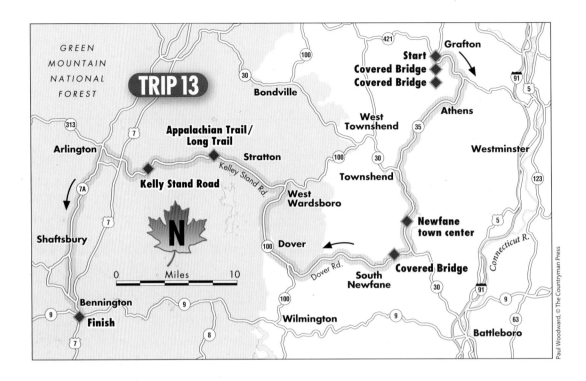

GREEN
MOUNTAIN
NATIONAL
FOREST

TRIP 13

Bondville

Arlington

Appalachian Trail/
Long Trail

Stratton

Kelly Stand Road

Kelley Stand Rd.

West
Wardsboro

Shaftsbury

N

Miles

0   10

Dover

Dover Rd.

South
Newfane

Bennington
Finish

Wilmington

West
Townshend

Townshend

Athens

Westminster

Start
Covered Bridge
Covered Bridge

Grafton

Newfane
town center

Covered Bridge

Battleboro

Connecticut R.

Paul Woodward, © The Countryman Press

Southern Vermont Odyssey: Classic Villages and Back Roads

The Trip: There are so many destination-worthy small villages in southern Vermont that it was hard for us to settle on just a few, but in the end it made sense to start this excursion with visits to Grafton and Newfane, two of the prettiest little towns in Vermont. After Newfane, the route follows a remote road through the heart of the southern Green Mountains on the way to Arlington, and a beautiful drive through farmland and mountain views to finish at Bennington, a bustling small city near the Massachusetts border. Bennington has numerous restaurants if you'd like to end this outing with lunch or dinner. Plan on half a day for this 45-mile trip, because you will undoubtedly be distracted along the way by the many photo ops, shops, art galleries, and hiking trails. After the trip, if you're heading back to the eastern edge of the state, we suggest taking VT 9, a quicker but still scenic route through the Green Mountains that will lead you to Brattleboro and the major north-south roads there: VT 5, VT 30, and I-91.

Basic Route: This trip follows VT 35 and VT 30 south from Grafton to Newfane. From Newfane, head west on Grimes Hill and Dover Roads to VT 100 north. It is an 8-mile drive on VT 100 to West Wardsboro and a road that is alternately called Arlington-Stratton Road, Stratton-Arlington Road, and Kelley Stand Road. This primarily gravel road works its way up and over a pass in the Green Mountains, reaching North Road in East Arlington in 17.5 miles. At the end of Kelley Stand Road, turn left on North Road, which turns into Kansas Road, then turn left on East Arlington Road in the center of East Arlington and follow it to Main Street (VT 7A) in Arlington and

Distance
45 miles one-way
Approximate Driving Time
1 hour 30 minutes
Peak Time
First and second weeks of October
Services
Grafton, Townshend, Arlington, Bennington
Fees
None

🔺 Historic Windham County Courthouse, Newfane, Vermont.

turn left. Follow VT 7A and VT 7 south to the end of the trip in Bennington.

Start: VT 35 and VT 121 in Grafton, Vermont. Grafton is the quintessential small New England village, with a charming lit- tle Main Street, several art galleries, a historic inn, and a great little café where you can grab a cup of coffee or a sandwich. It is a fun place to walk nearby trails past stone walls and woods. Part of the appeal of Grafton is well-preserved architecture and the fact that all the power and phone lines are underground (we photographers really appreciate that!). About a mile south of town on Grafton Road is the Grafton Village Cheese Company, where you can sample the goodies and visit the covered bridge next door.

◉ **GPS coordinates:**
N 42 42.021, W 73 6.826.

From Grafton head east/south on VT 35/VT 121 for a nice drive beside the rushing waters of the Saxtons River, then take a right on VT 35 south where VT 121 continues straight. VT 35 meanders through forests and farms for 10 miles to Townshend. From Townshend continue south on VT 30 to Newfane.

Hot Spot: Newfane, Vermont. There's not much to do in Newfane, but you will want to stop and admire the center of town with its beautiful trio of 19th-century white buildings: the town meetinghouse, the Congregational church, and the Windham County Courthouse. (Be sure to peek inside here—it looks like a scene right out of *Twelve Angry Men*.)

◉ **GPS coordinates:**
N 42 59.177, W 72 39.350.

Two miles south of Newfane, turn right onto Grimes Hill Road. The next several miles are a trip through Vermont at its most rural—small farms, woodlots, and fast-flowing streams. Two and a half miles

Stratton Mountain Leg Stretcher

This 6.8-mile strenuous hike takes four or five hours, so only embark on it if the weather is good, you are in hiking shape, and you get an early enough start. However, if you have the time and the energy, the 360-degree views of the Green Mountains from the fire tower at the mountain's summit are well worth the effort. The hike follows the white blazes of the Appalachian Trail/Long Trail north from a parking area on Stratton-Arlington Road, 8 miles west of VT 100. The 3.4-mile, 1,700-foot climb follows moderate grades for most of its length. From the fire tower the view stretches from the nearby Green Mountains to Mount Monadnock in New Hampshire, Mount Greylock in Massachusetts, and the Taconic Range in western New York.

◉ **GPS coordinates:**
N 43 33.666, W 72 58.090.

from VT 30, you will pass through a covered bridge in Dover, then bear right in 0.25 mile onto Dover Road. Dover Road winds its way though hill farm country for about 11 miles before running into VT 100 in West Dover. Take a right on VT 100, and drive north for 8 miles to West Wardsboro, then turn left onto Arlington-Stratton

🔺 Roaring Branch Brook in Sunderland, Vermont.

Hot Spot: Kelley Stand Road. After passing the Appalachian Trail, the road's name changes again to Kelley Stand Road and begins its descent to East Arlington. Kelley Stand Road is one of the prettiest forest roads in the state, especially during peak foliage when the beautiful stands of birch and maple line the roadsides and the fast-flowing waters of Roaring Branch Brook, a tributary of the Batten Kill River.

⊙ **GPS coordinates:**
N 43 3.083, W 73 4.542.

At the end of Kelley Stand Road, turn left on North Road, which soon turns into Kansas Road. In the center of the little town of East Arlington, turn left on East Arlington Road and follow it to VT 7A (Main Street); turn left again here and drive south for 13.6 miles. This road is busier than the others on the trip, but there are nice views of the Green Mountains to the east for most its length.

Finish: In Bennington, turn right on VT 7 for the 1-mile drive to downtown and the end of this trip at the intersection of VT 7 and VT 9.

⊙ **GPS coordinates:**
N 42 52.693, W 73 11.826.

Road, which soon becomes Stratton-Arlington Road. This road turns to gravel and soon leaves civilization behind, climbing through the forests of the Green Mountains to a pass near the trailhead to the Appalachian Trail. About 7.5 miles west of VT 100, the road passes a side road on the left that leads to Grout Pond, a pretty, undeveloped pond that's good for a quick foliage paddle if you happen to have a canoe or kayak with you.

TRIP 14

New Hampshire's Mount Monadnock

The Trip: This relatively short drive is a great tour of the classic rural New Hampshire landscapes found in the southwestern part of the state. White steepled churches and stone walls mix with farms and forests, all surrounding the 3,165-foot summit of Mount Monadnock. The mountain's modest elevation belies its prominence in a region of much shorter hills and gently rolling valley farms. The small towns of Peterborough and Jaffrey feature some homey restaurants, while Jaffrey Center shows off a picturesque town green, com-

plete with a historic cemetery and bright white church and meetinghouse. The trip ends with a drive up the summit of Pack Monadnock Mountain, where you can take in breathtaking foliage and sunset views from the fire tower. This route can be combined with Trip 15 for those wanting to make a day of it in this part of the state.

Basic Route: This trip begins in Peterborough, New Hampshire, and loops around Mount Monadnock by following NH 101 west, NH 137 south, NH 124 west, and NH 101 east back to Peterborough. It then continues east on NH 101 to the auto road in Miller State Park, ending on the summit of Pack Monadnock Mountain.

Start: US 202 and NH 101 in Peterborough, New Hampshire. Situated on the banks of the Contoocook River, Peterborough has a great little shopping district about half a mile north of this intersection on Grove Street. To start this drive, head west on NH 101.

⊙ **GPS coordinates:**
N 42 52.632, W 71 57.035.

Distance
45 miles round-trip
Approximate Driving Time
1 hour 15 minutes
Peak Time
First and second weeks of October
Services
Peterborough, Jaffrey, Marlborough, Dublin
Fees
$4 adults, $2 children for entrance to Miller State Park and Monadnock State Park

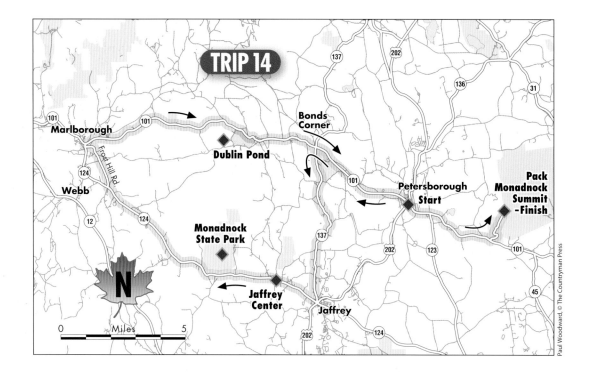

Paul Woodward. © The Countryman Press

Four and a half miles west of Peterborough, turn left on NH 137 for the 6.6-mile drive to NH 124 in Jaffrey; turn right on NH 124.

Hot Spot: Jaffrey Center. Two miles west of Jaffrey, Jaffrey Center is a small village that retains its 19th-century sensibilities. A large town green lined with stone walls serves as the foreground for a beautiful meetinghouse, complete with clock tower. The Old Burying Ground beside the meetinghouse contains the burial site of Willa Cather, author of *O Pioneers!* and *My Antonia*.

⊙ **GPS coordinates:**
N 42 49.726, W 72 3.426.

As you continue west on NH 124, the road weaves through woods and past a few farms with teasing views of Mount Monadnock to the north. Five miles west of Jaffrey Center you finally get an unobstructed view of the mountains as the road crosses Perkins Pond. In another 3.7 miles turn right onto Frost Hill Road for a short side trip that passes another view of Monadnock at the site of the old Marlborough Meeting House, now a field bordered by rock walls. Stay on Frost Hill Road for another 1.4 miles where it turns into Pleasant Street and reconnects with NH 124 in another 0.6 mile. Turn right on NH 124 then right on NH 101 in a few hundred yards.

Hot Spot: Dublin Pond. Seven miles west of NH 124, NH 101 follows closely along the shore of Dublin Pond. There are a couple of small pull-outs on the right where you can get some nice photographs of Mount Monadnock and the forest, brilliant with fall colors, across the lake. Shortly after the lake is the tiny center of Dublin, home to the most New England of publications, *Yankee Magazine.*

◉ **GPS coordinates:**
N 42 54.443, W 72 4.608.

Hot Spot: Pack Monadnock Mountain. About 7 miles west of Dublin, you will come to Peterborough, the starting point for this trip. Continue east on NH 101 for another 4 miles to the entrance to Miller State Park on the left. There is a paved auto road in the park that leads 1.4 miles up switchbacks to a parking lot on the summit. There are nice views to the north and east from the parking area, but the best views can be had by climbing the fire tower.

◉ **GPS coordinates:**
N 42 51.720, W 71 52.700.

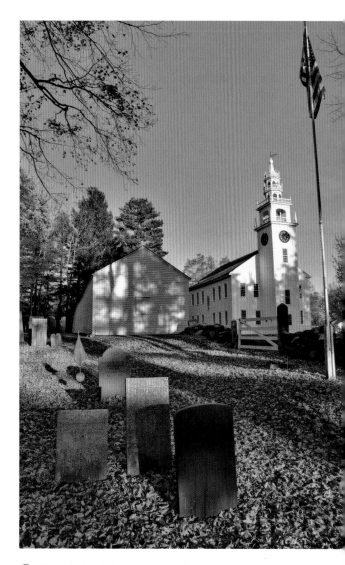

⬥ Old Burying Ground and Meetinghouse, Jaffrey Center.

Mt. Monadnock State Park
Leg Stretcher

▲ Mount Monadnock, Jaffrey, New Hampshire.

Mount Monadnock is widely claimed to be the most climbed mountain in the world. The mountain's interesting trails traverse open, rocky ledges from every direction, and its bald summit has unobstructed views stretching from Boston to the White Mountains. There are two campgrounds in the park, with the Gilson Pond Campground offering some of the best valley views of the mountain. If you want to climb the peak, check in at park head-quarters for trail maps and hike suggestions from the resident rangers. No matter which trail you choose, expect several hours of hiking on steep, rocky terrain. To get to park headquarters, turn right on Dublin Road, 0.3 mile west of Jaffrey Center, then turn left on Poole Road in another 1.3 miles. The park is at the end of Poole Road in about 0.5 mile.

◉ **GPS coordinates:**
N 42 50.742, W 72 5.282.

Covered Bridge Tour: Southwestern New Hampshire

The Trip: The small towns of extreme southwest New Hampshire boast a concentrated collection of covered bridges that make great destinations for a morning or afternoon foliage tour. This trip visits four bridges in the first 15 miles. All span the Ashuelot River, a whitewater tributary of the Connecticut that is one of only 15 or so rivers in the world that is home to the endangered dwarf wedge mussel (don't expect to see any unless you bring scuba gear and know exactly where to look!), a diminutive and nondescript freshwater bivalve. The second half of this trip takes you to the Chesterfield Gorge, views of the Connecticut River valley, and past Pisgah State Park, New Hampshire's largest state park at over 13,000 acres. Except for the few miles in and around the small city of Keene, there will be plenty of good hardwood forests bursting with color along the way.

Basic Route: This trip starts on NH 119 at the Ashuelot Covered Bridge, heads east to NH 10 north in Winchester, and then follows NH 10 to NH 101 in Keene. Along the way, there are three side trips to the Coombs, Thompson, and Sawyer's Crossing bridges. From Keene, the trip heads west on NH 101 and NH 9 to Chesterfield Gorge, then continues to NH 63. You will spend about 10 miles on NH 63 before turning left on NH 119 in Hinsdale to head back to the starting point at Ashuelot.

Start: Ashuelot Covered Bridge in Ashuelot, New Hampshire. This charming white bridge with a red roof is on NH 119, 3.6 miles east of NH 63. Built in 1864, the 159-foot bridge spans the Ashuelot River above a beautiful section of moderate whitewa-

Distance
40 miles round-trip
Approximate Driving Time
1 hour 10 minutes
Peak Time
Second week of October
Services
Keene, Hinsdale, Winchester
Fees
None

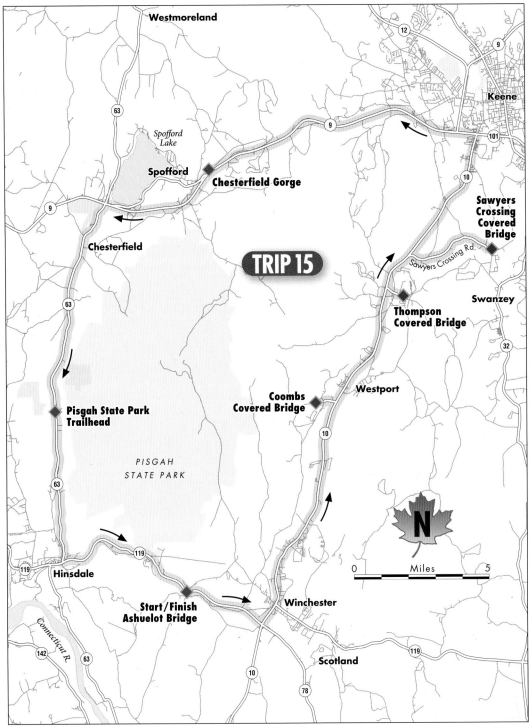

Westmoreland

Keene

Spofford
Lake

Spofford

Chesterfield Gorge

Sawyers
Crossing
Covered
Bridge

Chesterfield

TRIP 15

Sawyers Crossing Rd.

Swanzey

Thompson
Covered Bridge

Pisgah State Park
Trailhead

Coombs
Covered Bridge

Westport

PISGAH
STATE PARK

N

Miles

Hinsdale

Start/Finish
Ashuelot Bridge

Winchester

Connecticut R.

Scotland

Paul Woodward, © The Countryman Press

ter. During peak foliage there is good color on the hillside downstream from the river.

⊙ **GPS coordinates:**
N 42 46.648, W 72 25.389.

Hot Spot: Coombs Covered Bridge. From Ashuelot, follow NH 119 west for 2 miles, turning left on NH 10. As you head north on NH 10 from the town of Winchester, look for Coombs Bridge Road on the left, 5.5 miles north of NH 119. Coombs Bridge is at the end of this road in about 0.5 mile. Built in 1837, Coombs is a 118-foot-long unpainted wooden bridge with a red tin roof.

⊙ **GPS coordinates:**
N 42 50.291,W 72 21.562.

▼ Ashuelot Covered Bridge, Winchester, New Hampshire.

Coombs Covered Bridge, Winchester, New Hampshire.

Hot Spot: Thompson Covered Bridge. Another 3 miles north of Coombs Bridge Road on NH 10, turn right on California Street for the 0.2-mile drive to the Thompson Covered Bridge in West Swanzey. Built in 1864, the 136-foot-long bridge spans the Ashuelot in a small industrial part of West Swanzey that is less attractive than the quiet settings of the first two bridges on this trip. Still, this red-and-white bridge features attractive latticework that allows for good views of the river from the bridge itself.

◉ **GPS coordinates:**
N 42 52.294, W 72 19.637.

Hot Spot: Sawyer's Crossing Covered Bridge. The last bridge on our tour spans a quiet stretch of the Ashuelot in Swanzey, New Hampshire. Built in 1859, the bridge is 158 feet long and features a canoe put-in if you happen to have a boat and feel like a quiet paddle through fall foliage. The bridge is on Sawyer's Crossing Road, 2.1 miles east of NH 10, about 1 mile north of California Street.

◉ **GPS coordinates:**
N 42 53.203, W 72 17.220.

From Sawyer's Crossing, head back to NH 10 north and follow it for about 3 miles to the traffic circle in Keene; there, take the third exit onto NH 101 west. In another 0.4 mile, stay straight on what is now NH 9 west and follow that for 6 miles to the

Chesterfield Gorge State Wayside, which will be on your right.

Hot Spot: Chesterfield Gorge. From the parking area, you can hike down a short (but steep) trail to a wooden bridge that spans the small yet interesting Chesterfield Gorge. The gorge is still being carved by a small stream that drops 15 feet in a waterfall just below the footbridge. The cool air trapped by the gorge creates the perfect conditions for the grove of hemlocks that grow there. Scattered birch trees add a splash of yellow during foliage season.

⦿ GPS coordinates:
N 42 54.866, W 72 24.293.

About 3.5 miles beyond Chesterfield Gorge, turn left on NH 63 for the 8.5-mile drive to NH 119 in Hinsdale. You'll pass through the well-manicured center of Chesterfield and farms that provide good views west across the Connecticut River valley into southern Vermont. You will also pass a trailhead for hiking trails in Pisgah State Park (see "Mount Pisgah Leg Stretcher"). In Hinsdale, turn left to follow NH 119 back to Ashuelot to complete the loop.

Mount Pisgah Leg Stretcher

Near the end of this drive, you will pass a parking area for a trailhead in Pisgah State Park on NH 63, 4.5 miles south of NH 9. This is a great place to stop if you want to take a hike and explore the quiet woods of the park. There are two options here: a flat, 5-mile loop hike around Kilburn Pond, or a 4.5-mile hike to Mount Pisgah that gains about 500 feet of elevation. Though the summit is forested, there are excellent views of the surrounding forests and of Mount Monadnock from open ledges south of the summit. To start either hike, walk up the Kilburn Road for 0.7 mile to the Kilburn Loop Trail. If you opt for the loop around the pond, turn right here. For Mount Pisgah, go straight and then turn right in another 0.2 mile on the second intersection with the Kilburn Loop Trail. At 1.2 miles, turn left on the Pisgah Mountain Trail, then in another 0.4 miles, turn right on the Pisgah Ridge Trail and follow it for about 0.2 mile to the open ledges at Parker's Perch. This is where you'll get the best views of the hike, so you can either turn around here or hike the final 0.5 mile to the summit if you feel the need to "bag a peak." The up-and-back hike should take approximately two and a half hours.

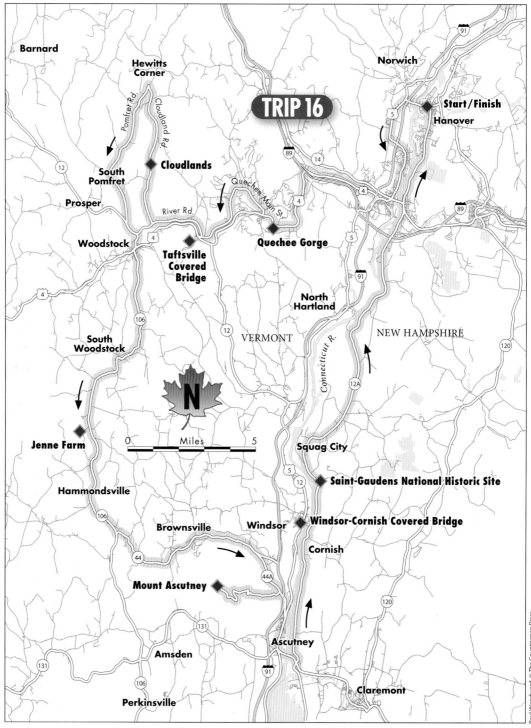

Barnard

Hewitts
Corner

Pomfret Rd.

Cloudland Rd.

TRIP 16

Norwich

91

5

◆ **Start/Finish**
Hanover

89

14

South
Pomfret

12

◆ **Cloudlands**

Quechee Main St.

4

4

89

Prosper

River Rd.

Woodstock

4

◆ **Taftsville Covered Bridge**

◆ **Quechee Gorge**

5

91

North
Hartland

4

NEW HAMPSHIRE

Connecticut R.

120

106

VERMONT

12

South
Woodstock

N

12A

0   Miles   5

◆ **Jenne Farm**

Squag City

Hammondsville

5

106

Saint-Gaudens National Historic Site ◆

Brownsville

Windsor

◆ **Windsor-Cornish Covered Bridge**

44

Cornish

44A

◆ **Mount Ascutney**

131

120

Amsden

Ascutney

131

91

106

Claremont

Perkinsville

Paul Woodward, © The Countryman Press

Connecticut River Upper Valley: New Hampshire and Vermont

The Trip: The exact borders of the Connecticut River's Upper Valley near Hanover, New Hampshire, are a little vague, but no matter how you draw it, the region includes some of New England's best scenery. This trip starts at the Dartmouth College green in Hanover and immediately crosses the river to explore the rural landscapes around Woodstock, Vermont. It then climbs to the views atop Mount Ascutney before crossing back into New Hampshire for a drive next to the river on the way back to Hanover. The area is dominated by winding river roads and rolling hills covered in northern hardwood forests that show off the fall foliage that draws visitors to New England. In addition, the towns along the way have that classic New England feel, with beautiful architecture, inviting main streets, and covered bridges, including the longest covered bridge in the U.S. Plan on spending half a day on this 90-mile loop drive.

Basic Route: This trip starts in Hanover and loops west and south in Vermont on US 5, US 4, VT 106, VT 44, and VT 12 before crossing the Connecticut River and returning via NH 12A and NH 10. In Quechee and Pomfret, Vermont, the route detours from US 4 to explore some great back roads—Quechee Main Street, River Road, Cloudland Road, and Pomfret Road.

Start: NH 10 and NH 10A in downtown Hanover, New Hampshire. Home to Dartmouth College, Hanover has a vibrant Main Street with bookstores, restaurants,

Distance
90 miles round-trip
Approximate Driving Time
2 hours 45 minutes
Peak Time
First and second weeks of October
Services
Hanover and Lebanon in New Hampshire; White River Junction, Quechee, and Woodstock in Vermont.
Fees
$3 per person for entrance to Ascutney State Park

🔺 A farm on Cloudland Road in Pomfret, Vermont.

and other diversions. The excellent Hood Museum of Art (http://hoodmuseum.dart-mouth.edu) is also a short walk from the beginning of this trip. Begin by driving west on NH 10A (Wheelock Street).

◉ **GPS coordinates:**
N 43 42.147, W 72 17.355.

After crossing the Connecticut River, turn left onto US 5 south and follow it for 5 miles through Wilder to White River Junction; turn right onto US 4 west.

Hot Spot: Quechee Gorge. Six miles from White River Junction, US 4 crosses a short bridge over Quechee Gorge, where there is a dramatic view of the Ottauquechee River, 165 feet below the steep cliffs of the gorge. There is parking at Quechee State Park on the left just before the gorge, where you can walk onto the bridge or hike a trail down to the river. There is also a parking area on the right, just west of the bridge.

◉ **GPS coordinates:**
N 43 38.238, W 72 24.502.

Less than a mile beyond the gorge, turn right on Waterman Hill Road for a short drive through the Quechee Covered Bridge to the village of Quechee, best known for its summer balloon festival and the Simon Pearce handblown glass gallery and restaurant. Turn left after the bridge onto Quechee Main Street, which parallels the Ottauquechee River for most of the 4 miles to the Taftsville Covered Bridge, a beautiful barn-red bridge built in 1836. Turn right before the bridge onto River Road.

Hot Spot: Cloudland Road. Just over 2 miles from the Taftsville bridge, turn right onto Cloudland Road. This narrow gravel road passes through the classic rural Vermont scenery shown on postcards—stone walls, red barns, gently rolling hills and fields. In spring, the roadside sugar maples don metal sap buckets. In fall, their bright orange leaves drape over the roadway.

◉ GPS coordinates:
N 43 39.493, 72 30.533.

Follow Cloudland Road 5 miles to its end, then turn right on Galaxy Hill Road (unmarked), which leads 0.7 miles back to

▼ The Connecticut River in Hartford, Vermont.

pavement. Turn left onto Pomfret Road (also unmarked), which follows Pomfret Brook past more farms and hills. When the road ends, in about 4 miles, turn left to stay on Pomfret Road, which ends at VT 12 in another 2 miles. Turn left on VT 12 south for the 2-mile drive into Woodstock.

Hot Spot: **Woodstock, Vermont.** Woodstock is one of our favorite villages in all of New England. It seems that every door on Elm, Central, and Pleasant Streets opens into a unique store, restaurant, or gallery. It also evinces the quintessential New England aesthetic, with its historic Woodstock Inn, town green, and Middle Covered Bridge. Just north of town on VT 12 are the beautiful grounds of the Marsh-Billings-Rockefeller National Historical Park (www .nps.gov/mabi/index.htm) and the Billings Farm and Museum, a working dairy farm that celebrates Vermont's rural heritage (www.billingsfarm.org).

◉ **GPS coordinates:**
N 43 37.519, W 72 31.110.

In Woodstock, follow the signs for VT 106, taking the U-turn around the town green and then turning right. VT 106 is yet another scenic route that passes rushing brooks, farms, and forests in hilly rural Vermont. Eight miles south of Woodstock you will pass Jenne Road, which leads to Jenne Farm, possibly the most photographed farm in all of New England—it is only a 0.25-mile detour if you want to take some snaps of your own. Thirteen miles south of Woodstock, turn left onto VT 44 east.

Hot Spot: **Mount Ascutney.** Seven miles east of VT 106, bear right onto VT 44A for the 1.8-mile drive to Mount Ascutney State Park ($3 entrance fee). The park has camping facilities and numerous hiking trails, and you can also drive the 3.5-mile auto road to 2,800 feet and excellent views of the surrounding countryside, including the nearby Connecticut River. To see the 360-degree views from the observation tower on the 3,144-foot high summit, you will need to hike the moderately strenuous 0.8-mile trail that leaves from the north end of the parking area.

◉ **GPS coordinates:**
N 43 26.385, W 72 27.100.

Hot Spot: **Cornish-Windsor Covered Bridge.** Continue on VT 44A south for another 1.2 miles and turn left onto VT 12 south, which crosses the Connecticut River back into New Hampshire; turn left on NH 12A north. In 5.5 miles, you will pass the Cornish-Windsor Covered Bridge, built in 1866. At 450 feet long, it is the longest covered bridge in the U.S., and the longest two-span covered bridge in the world.

◉ **GPS coordinates:**
N 43 28.411, W 72 22.944.

A mile and a half past the bridge is Saint-Gaudens National Historic Site, New Hampshire's only national park, which

🔺 The Cornish-Windsor Bridge.

preserves the home, gardens, and studios of the American sculptor Augustus Saint-Gaudens. NH 12A continues north, paralleling the Connecticut River for most of its length to the malls in West Lebanon and NH 10, 12.7 miles north of Saint-Gaudens. Turn left onto NH 10 for the 4-mile drive back to downtown Hanover.

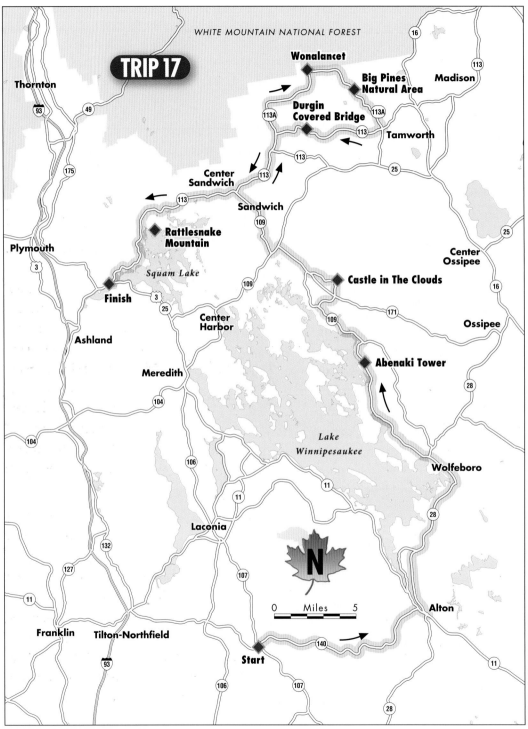

WHITE MOUNTAIN NATIONAL FOREST

TRIP 17

Thornton

93   49

175

Plymouth

3

Ashland

104

104

Wonalancet

Big Pines
Natural Area

Madison

113

16

Durgin
Covered Bridge

113A

113A

113

113

Tamworth

Center
Sandwich

113

Sandwich

113

25

113

109

Rattlesnake
Mountain

Squam Lake

109

Castle in The Clouds

Center
Ossipee

25

16

Finish

3

25

Center
Harbor

109

171

Ossipee

Meredith

Abenaki Tower

28

104

Lake
Winnipesaukee

Wolfeboro

106

11

11

28

Laconia

132

127

N

107

11

0   Miles   5

Alton

Franklin

Tilton-Northfield

Start

140

11

93

106

107

28

Paul Woodward, © The Countryman Press

New Hampshire's Lakes Region

The Trip: New Hampshire's Lakes Region was one of America's first tourist playgrounds in the mid-19th century, and for good reason. Its sparkling blue lakes are surrounded by fragrant pine and hardwood forests that cover the hills and mountains stretching from the Belknap Range south and west of Lake Winnipesaukee to the foot of the rugged White Mountains in the north. Today, the region is home to the touristy kitsch of Weirs Beach and traditional New England villages like Tamworth and Sandwich. This trip avoids the T-shirt shops and focuses on the natural beauty of the lakes and woods while also visiting some of the more scenic towns in the area. The drive will provide you with excellent lake and foliage views in between the towns, while also bringing you to a covered bridge and an oddity in New England—a castle. Foliage is excellent in most areas on this drive, as the green of white pines contrasts nicely with the orange, yellow, and red of the northern hardwood forests. Allow half a day for this excursion—though you could easily devote an entire day.

Distance
90 miles one-way
Approximate Driving Time
2 hours 45 minutes
Peak Time
Second and third weeks of October
Services
Alton, Wolfeboro, Moultonborough, Sandwich, Tamworth, Holderness
Fees
$5 for entrance to Castle in the Clouds preserve; $10 for entrance to castle

Basic Route: This trip follows all kinds of state routes and back roads as it meanders from Gilmanton southwest of Lake Winnipesaukee to Holderness on the northwest corner of Squam Lake. The details are in the trip description below, but you will basically be starting in Gilmanton and following NH 140, NH 11, NH 28A, NH 28, NH 109, NH 113, and NH 113A east, north, and west. There will be some detours off

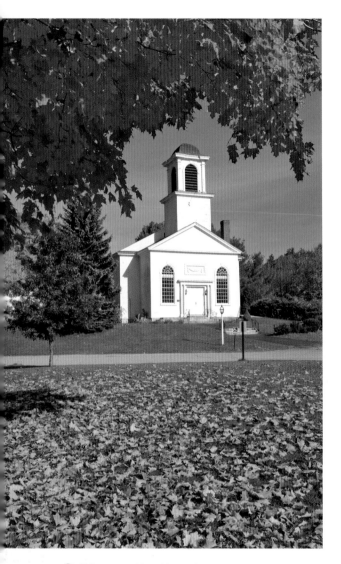

🔺 Gilmanton, New Hampshire.

of these routes to visit Castle in the Clouds in Moultonborough and the Durgin Covered Bridge in North Sandwich.

Start: NH 140 and NH 107 in downtown Gilmanton, New Hampshire. Gilmanton is small, with a convenience store and a beautiful town green, as well as some nice back roads to explore. To begin the trip, head east on NH 140 toward Alton.

⏺ **GPS coordinates:**
N 43 25.451, W 71 24.836.

The 12 mile-drive from Gilmanton to Alton is primarily one of beautiful rural and forested scenery that provides a great warm-up for the sweeping views of lakes and mountains that follow. In Alton, turn left on NH 11 and then turn right on NH 28A in about 1 mile, in Alton Bay. NH 28A follows the shoreline of Lake Winnipesaukee for 2 miles before jogging to the east and ending at NH 28. Turn left on NH 28 for the 7-mile drive to Wolfeboro, the self-proclaimed "Oldest Summer Resort in America." You will definitely want to take the time to park and explore Main Street and the waterfront, with its excellent views of the lake.

Hot Spot: Abenaki Tower. From Wolfeboro, continue north on NH 109, which passes more lakeside views to the entrance to Abenaki Tower on the right, 8.5 miles north of NH 28. The tower has excellent views of the surrounding lakes and mountains.

⏺ **GPS coordinates:**
N 43 40.235, W 71 17.530.

From the tower, continue north on NH 109 for another 4.7 miles, and turn right on

Severance Road, which leads 1.2 miles to NH 171, Old Mountain Road.

Hot Spot: Castle in the Clouds. Turn left on NH 171, then right into Castle in the Clouds (www.castleintheclouds.org) in about 0.2 mile. Castle in the Clouds was the early-20th-century estate of shoe magnate Thomas Plant and his wife, Olive.

Their home, Lucknow, is a beautiful example of New England Arts and Crafts architecture and is perched high atop a ridge in the Ossipee Mountains with dramatic views of the Lakes Region. In 2003 the estate was purchased and preserved by the Lakes Region Conservation Trust, which provides public access to Lucknow and 5,500 acres of forests, fields, and water-

▼ Maple tree, Castle in the Clouds.

falls. The 45 miles of hiking trails and carriage roads offer good opportunities to get out of the car and explore the woods and streams on foot. There are also great views from the road itself as it winds up the mountain to the estate and then back down to NH 171 past Shannon Pond.

◉ GPS coordinates:
N 43 43.573, W 71 19.503.

When you get back to NH 171, turn right and follow it for about 0.5 mile to NH 109; follow 109 north for 2.2 miles to NH 25 in Moultonborough. Turn left, then turn right in 0.6 mile to continue on NH 109 north. In 4.5 miles you will reach the charming little village of Center Sandwich, with its maple-lined town green and general store. Turn right on NH 113A, Maple Street.

Hot Spot: **Wonalancet Village.** Just over 3.5 miles north of Center Sandwich, continue straight on NH 113A for 3 miles to the tiny village of Wonalancet. There's not much to do here, but the white steepled church set against a backdrop of foliage and the Sandwich Range of the White Mountains offers a prime New England photo op.

◉ GPS coordinates:
N 43 54.466, W 71 20.934.

Hot Spot: **Big Pines Natural Area.** Continuing past Wonalancet, NH 113A meanders through beautiful mature woods in the Hemenway State Forest, reaching the Big Pines Natural Area in 3.7 miles. Park in the lot on the right and make the walk to the pedestrian bridge over the rushing waters of the Swift River. The fall colors are less brilliant here, but the 150-year-old white pines (the largest is 42 inches in diameter) make up for it.

◉ GPS coordinates:
N 43 53.261, W 71 17.621.

Three miles beyond Big Pines brings you to Tamworth, another beautiful little village, complete with stone-wall-lined fields, a steepled church, general store, and mountain views. Turn right on Main Street, which soon turns to dirt as it becomes Cleveland Hill Road, named after President Grover Cleveland, who summered here.

Hot Spot: **Durgin Covered Bridge.** Follow Cleveland Hill Road for about 5 miles as it winds through forests, fields, and views of the surrounding mountains to Bridge View Road. Turn left, and follow this narrow dirt road for about 0.5 mile to the Durgin Covered Bridge, built in 1869 to span the Cold River.

◉ GPS coordinates:
N 43 51.355, W 71 21.848.

Once across the bridge turn right on Fellows Hill Road, which brings you back to NH 113A in 1.4 miles. Follow NH 113A south to North Sandwich; continue straight on NH 113 for another 4 miles back to Center Sandwich.

Finish: NH 113 and NH 25 in Holderness. In Center Sandwich, turn right on NH 113 (Main Street) for a rolling 12-mile drive to the end of this trip at the intersection of NH 113, NH 25, and US 3 in Holderness, near the northwestern corner of Squam Lake. A left on US 3/NH 25 brings you to the little village of Holderness on the banks of the river that connects Squam Lake and Little Squam Lake. Check out the nearby Squam Lakes Natural Science Center (www.nhnature.org).

◉ **GPS coordinates:**
N 43 43.868, W 71 35.154.

🔺 View of Squam Lake from West Rattlesnake Hill.

Rattlesnake Mountain Leg Stretcher

The Rattlesnakes are a pair of rocky hills that quickly rise about 700 feet above the coves on the eastern end of Squam Lake. There are numerous trails to both summits, with the Old Bridle Path being the easiest way up to West Rattlesnake, which has spectacular views to the south and west of the lake and surrounding hardwood forests. The summit is rocky and sparsely populated by scrubby oak trees and twisted pitch pines. The trail is wide and easy to follow for its entire length (about 1 mile, with a 400-foot ascent). Expect the hike to take about 1.5 hours up and back. The trailhead is on the south side of NH 113, 6.3 miles from Center Sandwich. Parking is available in a lot on the north side of the street.

◉ **GPS coordinates:**
N 43 47.352, W 71 32.916.

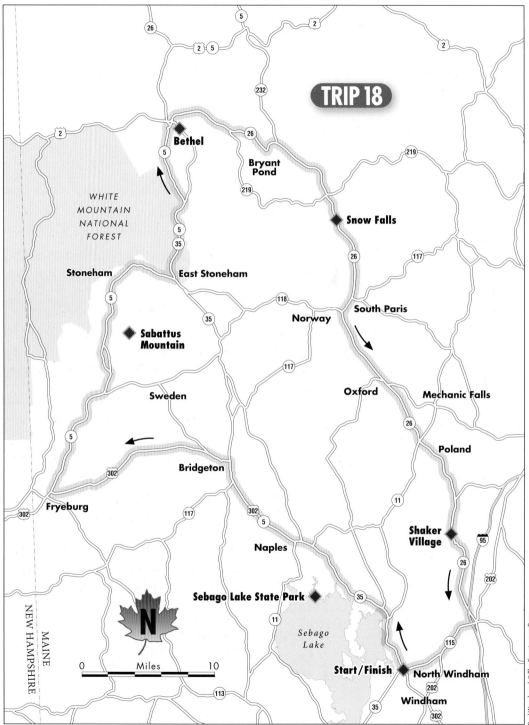

TRIP 18

Bethel

Bryant Pond

Snow Falls

WHITE
MOUNTAIN
NATIONAL
FOREST

Stoneham

East Stoneham

South Paris

Norway

Sabattus
Mountain

Sweden

Oxford

Mechanic Falls

Poland

Bridgeton

Fryeburg

Shaker
Village

Naples

Sebago Lake State Park

N

Sebago
Lake

NEW HAMPSHIRE
MAINE

0   Miles   10

Start/Finish   North Windham

Windham

Paul Woodward, © The Countryman Press

Maine's Western Lakes Region

The Trip: This 130-mile, day-long drive starts just outside of Portland, but it quickly leaves the city behind, cruising past views of Sebago and Long lakes in Maine's popular western lakes region. As the trip heads north, it takes on a decidedly woodsy feel as it skirts the eastern edge of the White Mountain National Forest before reaching Bethel, Maine, a cozy little ski village, complete with the requisite shops, hotels, and restaurants. Returning south from Bethel, you will encounter a big swath of Maine farmland, culminating in the Sabbathday Lake Shaker Village, the sect's last working village, where you can shop for Shaker goods and tour the grounds. This trip features the northern hardwood forests of birch, beech, and maple that make fall in New England famous.

Basic Route: This trip starts in North Windham, Maine, and makes a big loop in a counterclockwise direction, following US 302 west, ME 5 north, ME 26 south, ME 26A south, and ME 115 west, which takes you back to North Windham.

Start: US 302 and ME 115 in North Windham, Maine. This is prime suburban-strip-mall territory. To get to the good stuff, drive west (north) on US 302.

⦿ GPS coordinates:
N 43 50.027, W 70 26.284.

Distance	
130 miles round-trip	
Approximate Driving Time	
3 hours 45 minutes	
Peak Time	
Second and third weeks of October	
Services	
Windham, Naples, Fryeburg, Bethel, Poland	
Fees	
$6.50 per adult to tour Sabbathday Lake Shaker Village	

🔺 Sunset over the Androscoggin River, Bethel, Maine.

The first 15 miles or so on US 302 between North Windham and Naples is busy, but you will be rewarded with the occasional lake views, and you can make a side trip to Sebago Lake State Park ($6.50) by following the state park road on the left, 11.4 miles into the drive. Naples has several trendy restaurants and sits on the edge of Long Lake. As the trip continues from here, the hustle and bustle dissipates and the trip gets more woodsy, particularly after US 302 bends left in Bridgton. There are some great views of foliage on this segment of the trip, particularly where the road crosses the Saco River. When you reach ME 5 just outside of Fryeburg, turn right for the drive to Bethel.

ME 5 continues driving through forests as it passes through the small village of Lovell on its way to Bethel, about 36 miles north of US 302. The foliage in and around Lovell is possibly the best of the entire loop.

Hot Spot: Bethel, Maine. The village core of Bethel is one of the prettiest in Maine's north country, its mix of cafés, shops, and inns more reminiscent of coastal Maine tourist towns than the typical northern Maine blue-collar town. The nearby Sunday River ski area drives much of the economic activity, but the town is lively year-round. The state roads bypass the center of town, so to get there you need to turn right off of ME 5 onto Mill Hill Road, about 0.5 mile south of US2/ME 26.

⊙ **GPS coordinates:**
N 44 24.338, W 70 47.402.

From Bethel, follow ME 26 south for the return trip to North Windham. On this leg of the journey, colorful forests are interspersed with more and more farmland as you head south through the little villages of Woodstock, South Paris, Norway, Poland, and New Gloucester.

Hot Spot: Snow Falls. About 18 miles south of Bethel, look for the Snow Falls Rest Area on the right side of the road in West Paris. You can park here and walk to the footbridge over the Little Androscoggin River, which plunges about 25 feet over a series of cascades in a narrow gorge. The river is lined with a mix of dark green hemlocks and colorful northern hardwoods.

⊙ **GPS coordinates:**
N 44 18.198, W 70 32.302.

Sabattus Mountain Leg Stretcher

The drive through Lovell is beautiful, but the forest is so thick it is hard to see anything but trees. A hike up nearby Sabattus Mountain will remedy that by taking you to some big views relatively quickly via a 1.5-mile loop trail. The trail climbs about 450 feet to the summit. Though the summit is only 1,150 feet above sea level, the landscape to the south drops off dramatically, giving great southern and eastern views of nearby lakes, mountains, and forests. Expect the hike to take about an hour. To get to the trailhead, look for Sabattus Road on the right off ME 5, 4.5 miles north of Lovell Road (ME 93). Follow Sabattus Road for 1.5 miles, then turn right onto Sabattus Mountain Road. Trailhead parking will be on the right in 0.6 mile.

⊙ **GPS coordinates:**
N 42 11.295, W 70 51.198.

🔺 Snow Falls, West Paris, Maine.

Hot Spot: Sabbathday Lake Shaker Village. This Shaker village in New Gloucester, Maine, is the only active and functioning Shaker community in the world. The Sabbathday Lake community was established in 1783, and six of the remaining 18 structures are open to the public. There is also a Shaker store and library, and extensive grounds that include working fields, orchards, woods, and shoreline on Sabbathday Lake. Guided tours are available Monday through Saturday, from Memorial Day through Columbus Day (www.shaker.lib.me.us). You will find the village on ME 26, 45 miles south of Bethel.

⦿ **GPS coordinates:**
N 43 59.173, W 70 21.995.

To complete the trip, follow ME 26 south for an additional 7 miles, turning right on ME 26A, and right again in another mile on ME 115. It is another 6.5 miles to US 302 in North Windham.

Southern Berkshires: Hay Fields, Waterfalls, and Cobbles

The Trip: Two loops in one trip show off the best of southern Berkshire County—charming villages, pastoral landscapes, and picturesque wild places. The trip begins in Stockbridge, Massachusetts, the longtime home of Norman Rockwell, and heads south through the bustling town of Great Barrington before exploring the fields and forests in and around Mount Washington State Forest. After a visit to probably the best-known waterfall in Massachusetts—Bash Bish Falls—the trip loops back through Great Barrington before heading east and looping through the little

towns of New Marlborough, Monterey, and Tyringham, site of Tyringham Cobble, a small rocky hill that juts up from the surrounding farms and offers great views of the fall foliage that peaks in mid-October. The forest here is southern New England hardwoods; oaks and beech trees turn gold and bronze and mix with a smattering of orange and red maples. Expect to spend about half a day to fully enjoy this 65-mile drive.

Basic Route: This trip begins in downtown Stockbridge, follows US 7 south through Great Barrington to MA 23 west. A short jaunt on MA 41 south brings you to Mount Washington Road and a series of additional back roads that meander for about 11 miles through the state forest to Bash Bish Falls. The trip continues into New York on NY 344, then heads back north on NY 22 to NY/MA 23 east, which brings you back to Great Barrington. Drive north through town on US 7, then head east on MA 23 to MA 57 south. Six miles later in New Marlborough, turn left on New Marl-

Distance
65 miles round-trip
Approximate Driving Time
2 hours 15 minutes
Peak Time
Second and third weeks of October
Services
Stockbridge, Great Barrington
Fees
None

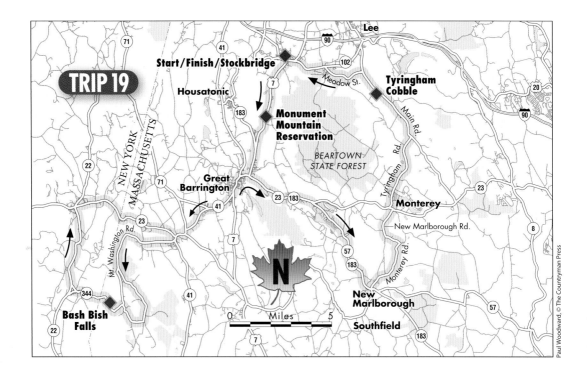

boro–Monterey Road, for the journey on back roads through Monterey to Tyringham. In Tyringham, turn left on Main Street, then left on Meadow Street. Meadow Street ends at MA 102; a left on MA 102 brings you back to Stockbridge.

Start: US 7 and MA 102 in Stockbridge, Massachusetts. Stockbridge still looks much like it did when Norman Rockwell painted here in the mid-20th century. The iconic Red Lion Inn stands in the center of town and the small general store featured in Rockwell's work is still on Main Street.

The Norman Rockwell Museum (www .nrm.org/) is about 2.5 miles west of town and is well worth the visit.

◉ **GPS coordinates:**
N 42 16.971, W 73 18.745.

◉Follow US 7 south from Stockbridge for about 8 miles, past the imposing cliffs of Monument Mountain and through the center of Great Barrington to MA 23; turn right on MA 23. In 4 miles, turn left on MA 41, then make the first right onto Mount Washington Road. The road soon leaves most houses behind, cruising through beautiful forests and past hay fields. After about 4.5 miles, the name of the road changes to East Street (follow the sign to Bash Bish Falls); turn right on Cross Street in another 3.5 miles. Cross Street becomes West Street before you will need to turn left on Bash Bish Falls Road, about 1.8 miles from East Street

(again, follow the sign to Bash Bish Falls.)

Hot Spot: Bash Bish Falls. After about 2 miles on Bash Bish Falls Road, you will reach a parking area for the falls on the left. There are two trails here. The first is a five-minute climb to a nice overlook of the

🔻 Fall colors reflected in a pond in Tyringham, Massachusetts.

🔺 Bash Bish Falls, the highest waterfall in Massachusetts.

forest in the steep, narrow valley below the falls. The second leads down 300 feet to the base of the falls over about 0.25 mile. With an 80-foot drop, the falls are the state's highest and can make for a dramatic photo in high water. The climb back up to the parking area is steep. There is a second parking area 1 mile south that is the trailhead for a flat 1-mile walk to the falls.

◉ **GPS coordinates:**
N 42 6.897, W 73 29.508.

Continuing on Bash Bish Falls Road leads to NY 344 in Copake Falls, New York. Follow NY 344 to NY 22 and turn right, then drive the 4 miles to NY/MA 23. Follow NY/MA 23 east back to Great Barrington and US 7 north. This being the midway point of the drive, you might want to take advantage of Great Barrington's tantalizing mix of restaurants, coffee shops, and cafés and grab a bite. North of town, turn right to follow MA 23 east for 3.5 miles to MA 57; turn right. In 6 miles you will come to the small village of New Marlborough; turn left on New Marlborough–Monterey Road, a classic New England back road that narrows as it travels past stone walls, farms, and forests reminiscent of Vermont. Three miles north of New Marlborough, turn left on New Marlborough Road, then turn right at the T intersection in another 0.8 mile.

▷ Old farm structure, Mount Washington State Forest.

Monument Mountain Leg Stretcher

While Bash Bish Falls and Tyringham Cobble both offer the opportunity to get some good exercise, Monument Mountain provides a slightly more challenging hike to the most dramatic views in the region. Located on the west side of US 7 about 3 miles south of Stockbridge, the mountain rises quickly from the valley floor, topping out at 1,640 feet on Squaw Peak. Spectacular views are found from numerous viewpoints on the mountain. Several trails make various trips possible. We like the loop made by following the Hickey Trail to the peak and then using the Indian Monument Trail for the return trip. This makes for a 2.1-mile loop that takes about an hour and a half to complete. Trail maps are usually available at the parking area, or you can get them ahead of time by contacting the Trustees of Reservations (www.thetrustees.org).

◉ **GPS coordinates:**
N 42 14.574, W 73 20.113.

New Marlborough Road ends at MA 23 in another quiet little village, Monterey. Turn left, then take a quick right onto Tyringham Road. Another 4 miles of beautiful rural scenery brings you to Main Street in Tyringham, yet another small village that will have you reaching for your camera.

Hot Spot: Tyringham Cobble. This preserve, managed by the Massachusetts Trustees of Reservations, includes 2 miles of trails that explore the area's meadows and forested "cobble," a small hill that rises about 400 feet above the surrounding fields and river valley. A section of the Appalachian Trail passes over the summit and past several rock outcroppings offering good views of the valley. To get to the preserve, turn left on Jerusalem Road from Main Street, 1.5 miles west of Tyringham Road. The parking area will be on the right in 0.2 mile.

◉ **GPS coordinates:**
N 42 14.584, W 73 12.327.

To complete the drive, continue west on Main Street, turning left on Meadow Street 2.7 miles west of Jerusalem Road. Meadow Street will take you 2.3 miles to MA 102; turn left on MA 102 for the 2-mile drive back to Stockbridge.

Pioneer Valley Vistas: Massachusetts's Connecticut River Tour

The Trip: Massachusetts's Pioneer Valley was one of the first regions of the country to be settled during European colonization, its fertile land adjacent to the waters of the Connecticut River being the main attraction. Although early settlers enjoyed the productive soils, they endured nearly a century of attacks from Native Americans, with some settlements being completely destroyed and others rebuilt in more strategic locations. This trip starts in Historic Deerfield, a living-history museum that preserves many of the homes from this early time period and is a great place to discover the details of life here in the 17th, 18th, and 19th centuries. The rest of this trip provides spectacular views of the river, valley farms, and surrounding hills from three mountain summits accessible by car—Mounts Sugarloaf, Holyoke, and Tom. The foliage here is a mix of northern hardwoods and southern New England hardwoods, providing a broad array of colors.

Basic Route: This trip follows US 5 south from Deerfield, to MA 116 south to Mount Sugarloaf and Sunderland. It then follows the Connecticut River on MA 47 south through Hadley and South Hadley to MA 116 south, then US 202 south in Holyoke. Finally, it heads north on US 5 to the Mount Tom State Reservation. It also follows the three auto roads up the mountains listed above.

Distance
40 miles one-way
Approximate Driving Time
1 hour 30 minutes
Peak Time
Second and third weeks of October
Services
Deerfield, Hadley, Holyoke
Fees
$2 (each attraction) for entrance to Mount Sugarloaf and Mount Tom State Reservations, and Skinner State Park.

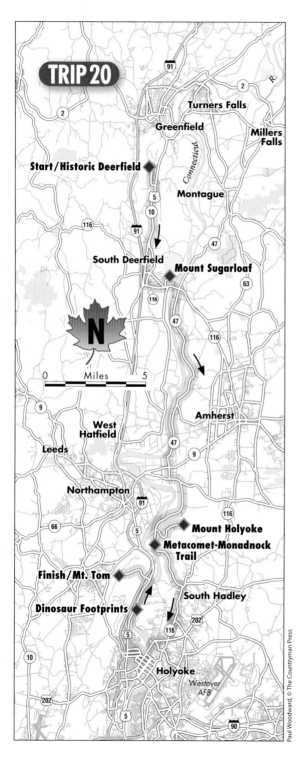

Paul Woodward, © The Countryman Press

Start: Old Main Street in Deerfield, Massachusetts. Historic Deerfield (www.historic-deerfield.org/) is one of the premier living-history museums in all of New England. You can walk Old Main Street and a trail along the Deerfield River for no charge, or buy a pass ($12 for adults, $5 for kids) to the museum buildings at the visitor center across the street from the post office. Old Main Street is 4.4 miles south of the intersection of US 5 and MA 2A in Greenfield.

⦿ **GPS coordinates:**
N 42 32.696, W 72 36.292.

From the Historic Deerfield visitor center, head south on Old Main Street, following it for 0.7 mile to US 5; turn right on US 5.

Hot Spot: Mount Sugarloaf. Five miles south of Historic Deerfield, turn left on MA 116 south. In 2 miles, the Mount Sugarloaf State Reservation will be on the left. Follow the auto road to the summit for commanding views of the Connecticut River valley. On the southern horizon, the river squeezes through Mount Holyoke and Mount Tom, the other two summits on this trip.

⦿ **GPS coordinates:**
N 42 28.291, W 72 35.503.

Continuing on MA 116 south, you will soon cross the river. After the river, turn right on MA 47 south for a nice drive through an interesting mix of historic tobacco farms, homes, and barns, and a bit of suburban sprawl. Tobacco was once the largest cash crop in the state, and the Pioneer Valley was the hub of the industry. About 10 miles south of MA 116, cross MA 9 and continue on MA 47. (Turning left on MA 9 will bring you to the malls in Hadley.)

Hot Spot: Mount Holyoke. Just over 4 miles south of MA 9, turn left, following the signs to the summit in Skinner State Park. The 2-mile road climbs switchbacks up to the summit, where you can check out the sweeping views of the river valley from the porch of the Skinner Mountain House,

🔻 Strawberry field and tobacco barn with view of Mount Sugarloaf.

Mount Holyoke Leg Stretcher

A good alternative to driving the road up Mount Holyoke is the 1.6-mile hike up to the summit via the Metacomet-Monad-nock Trail. The M-M Trail starts in central Connecticut and follows ridgelines adjacent to the Connecticut River before veering east and ending on Mount Monadnock in southwestern New Hampshire. To get to this section of the trail, follow MA 47 south from the auto road for 0.9 mile and turn left on Old Mountain Road. The trailhead will be on the right in about 0.1 mile. The trail starts with a short, steep climb before making a moderate ascent to the summit, passing several rock outcrops with good views to the west. From the summit, you can either retrace your steps back to the trailhead or make a loop following the red-blazed Dry Brook Trail, which descends the eastern slope of the mountain before turning west and returning to the M-M Trail close to the start of the hike. The hike should take about two hours.

● **GPS coordinates:**
N 42 17.341, W 72 36.105.

a popular hotel during the 1800s. This is where Thomas Cole made his famous painting of the Connecticut River oxbow.

● **GPS coordinates:**
N 42 18.033, W 72 35.257.

After visiting Mount Holyoke, make your way back down to MA 47 and continue south for about 3 miles, turning right on MA 116 south, then right again in 2.5 miles on US 202 south. US 202 crosses the river and passes through the industrial and blue-collar neighborhoods of Holyoke before reaching US 5, about 2.5 miles south of MA 116.

Finish: Mount Tom. Turn right on US 5 and follow it for 3.6 miles to Reservation Road on the left. This road leads 2 miles to a parking lot near the summit of Mount Tom. There are two lookout towers accessible from the parking area. Our favorite is the one on Goat Peak, which looks east across the river to Mount Holyoke and north to the oxbow. Another nearby place to visit is the Massachusetts Trustees of Reservations' Dinosaur Footprints Reservation, a short distance south of Reservation Road. Here you can walk down to the river and check out fossilized dinosaur footprints in the bedrock.

● **GPS coordinates:**
N 42 16.323, W 72 37.854.

TRIP 21

Not Far from Boston: Central Massachusetts

The Trip: Often overlooked during foliage season as tourists flock to the Berkshires, Green Mountains, and White Mountains, the region between Boston's western suburbs and the Connecticut River valley provides great foliage-viewing opportunities and requires much less driving from Boston than the more popular foliage tours. This trip starts with a visit to the summit of Mount Wachusett and its 360-degree views, then explores the quiet roads and sleepy villages between Wachusett and the Quabbin Reservoir in Ware. It ends with a great overlook of the forests and waters of the Quabbin. Foliage tends to

Distance
50 miles one-way
Approximate Driving Time
1 hour 40 minutes
Peak Time
Second or third week of October
Services
Barre, Petersham, Ware
Fees
$4 to walk the trails at Wachusett Meadow Wildlife Sanctuary

start a little earlier at Mount Wachusett than it does in the valleys and at Quabbin, but a visit during the middle of October should turn up good color at several points along the way. For the most part, the forests are dominated by oaks, hickories, and maples, with the odd conifer and birch tree mixed in depending on elevation and soil type. With all the great walks available along the way, you can easily spend the whole day making this trip. If you are in or near Boston and want to drive back roads the entire day, you can head to Wachusett by taking the following route: MA 2 west to MA 62 west in Concord to MA 117 west in Maynard to MA 110 south in Bolton to MA 62 west in Clinton to Mountain Road in Princeton.

Basic Route: This trip starts at the Wachusett State Reservation on Mountain Road in Princeton, with a drive up the auto road to the summit. Heading back down to the base of the mountain, the trip follows Mountain Road south to MA 62, then on to MA 32 north in Barre. In Petersham the trip follows back roads to 32A south and

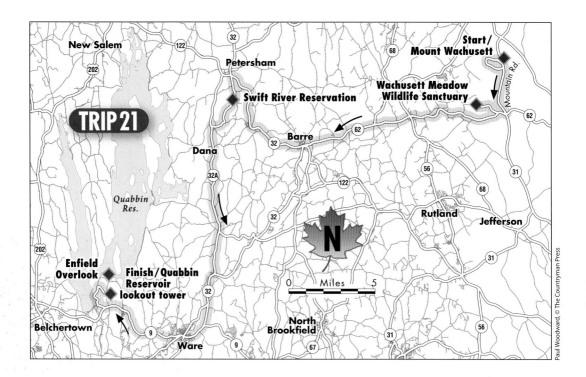

New Salem · 122 · 32 · Petersham · 202 · TRIP 21 · Swift River Reservation · Dana · 32 · Barre · 62 · 32A · 122 · Quabbin Res. · 56 · 31 · 68 · 32 · Rutland · Jefferson · 202 · 31 · Enfield Overlook · Finish/Quabbin Reservoir lookout tower · 32 · 0 Miles 5 · Belchertown · 9 · North Brookfield · 31 · 56 · Ware · 9 · 67 · Start/ Mount Wachusett · 68 · Wachusett Meadow Wildlife Sanctuary · Mountain Rd. · 62

Paul Woodward. © The Countryman Press

MA 32 south to MA 9 in Ware. Turn right on MA 9 west, which will take you to the Quabbin Reservoir's Winsor Dam entrance in 7.5 miles.

Start: Wachusett Mountain State Reservation in Princeton, Massachusetts. The easiest way to get to Wachusett and the base of the auto road is to take Exit 25 on MA 2 and head south on MA 140. Two miles from the exit, turn right on Mile Hill Road. In another 0.8 mile, stay left, following a sign for Wachusett Reservation (Mountain Road). The entrance to the park will be on the right in 0.2 mile. To get to the visitor center, turn left. For the sum-

mit, turn right for a 2.5-mile drive to the summit parking lot. There are several good viewpoints on ledges around the summit, and a nice view of Mount Monadnock in New Hampshire from the top of the ski lift down a short trail on the north side of the summit.

⦿ GPS coordinates:
N 42 29.320, W 71 53.215.

From the entrance to Wachusett, head south on Mountain Road past some sweeping east-facing views to the town green of Princeton, turning right on MA 62 and turning right again in 0.7 mile on Goodnow Road.

Hot Spot: Wachusett Meadow Wildlife Sanctuary. After about a mile on Goodnow Road, you will reach Massachusetts Audubon's Wachusett Meadow Wildlife Sanctuary, 1,200 acres of fields, woods, and wetlands that includes 12 miles of hiking trails. This is one of our favorite preserves in Massachusetts, and it is well worth a few hours of walking and wildlife watching. The sanctuary's 1,300-foot summit is a great place to watch for migrating hawks in the fall, especially on a clear day following a storm when the birds take advantage of winds out of the northwest to make their way south for the winter.

◉ **GPS coordinates:**
N 42 27.324, W 71 54.308.

▼ Forest scene, Quabbin Reservoir.

After visiting the sanctuary, head back to MA 62 and drive west for about 12.5 miles to MA 32 in Barre. Much of MA 62 has a backwoods feel, as the road is narrow and trees encroach, their overhanging branches adding plenty of color to the drive. In Barre, turn right on MA 32 toward Petersham for 7.5 miles. Here MA 32 turns right for a short drive to Petersham center and its beautiful town green and general store. Instead, this trip turns left on South Street toward the Swift River Reservation.

Hot Spot: Swift River Reservation. Like the Wachusett Meadow Reservation, this preserve (managed by the Massachusetts Trustees of Reservations) features miles of trails through meadows and woods. Our favorite part of the reservation is the walk along the east branch of the Swift River, where mature forest overhangs the rocks in the fast-flowing river. To get to the reservation, follow South Street for 1 mile and turn right on Nichewaug Road. Parking will be on the left in 0.7 mile.

◉ **GPS coordinates:**
N 42 27.603, W 72 10.937.

To make the drive toward Quabbin, continue on Nichewaug Road for another 1.5 miles and turn right on Glen Valley Road, following this road to its end at Hardwick Road (MA 32A). Turn left on MA 32A and follow it south through the forests east of Quabbin for 2.5 miles, turning right on MA 32 in Gilbertville. Another 3.5 miles brings you to MA 9 in Ware; head west by turning right on MA 9.

Hot Spot: Quabbin Reservoir. About 7.5 miles west of Ware is the Winsor Dam entrance to the Quabbin Reservoir, which at 18 miles long and with 181 miles of shoreline is the largest lake in Massachusetts. Created by damming the Swift River in 1936, the reservoir flooded four towns, Dana, Enfield, Greenwich, and Prescott, in order to provide drinking water for Boston and 40 surrounding communities. The area around Quabbin is primarily wilderness, as the state restricts development on several thousand acres of surrounding forest in order to preserve water quality. The reservoir is now a wintering ground for dozens of bald eagles, and it is possible to spot them during the fall as well. There are several good spots to view the reservoir from the road (the Enfield Overlook, about 2.2 miles from the entrance, is our favorite), and there are big 360-degree views from the lookout tower on Quabbin Hill. To reach the tower, turn right at the traffic circle, 1.8 miles from MA 9.

◉ **GPS coordinates:**
N 42 17.941, W 72 19.954.

PART IV
Coastal Byways

Dawn over the Atlantic, Brenton Point State Park, Newport, Rhode Island.

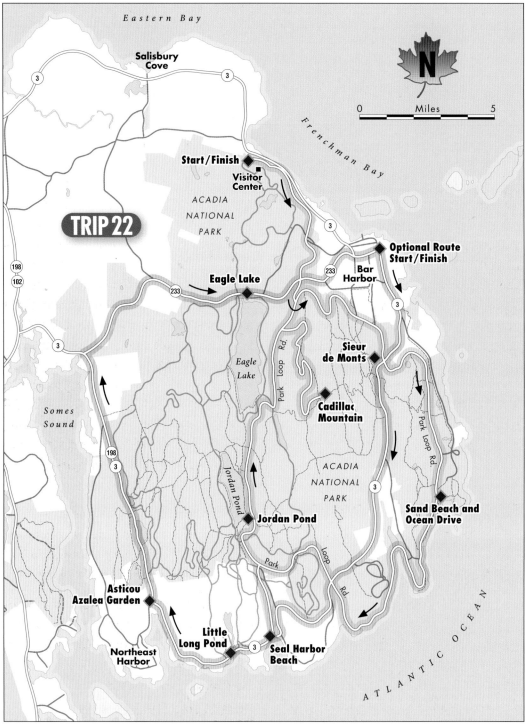

Eastern Bay

Salisbury Cove

3

3

N

0   Miles   5

Frenchman Bay

Start/Finish
Visitor Center

ACADIA NATIONAL PARK

TRIP 22

3

Optional Route Start/Finish

198
102

233

Bar Harbor

Eagle Lake

233

3

Sieur de Monts

Eagle Lake

Park Loop Rd.

Cadillac Mountain

3

ACADIA NATIONAL PARK

Park Loop Rd.

Somes Sound

198
3

Jordan Pond

Sand Beach and Ocean Drive

3

Jordan Pond

Park   Loop

Asticou Azalea Garden

Rd.

Northeast Harbor

Little Long Pond

3

Seal Harbor Beach

ATLANTIC OCEAN

Paul Woodward. © The Countryman Press

Acadia National Park Loop Road

The Trip: Acadia National Park's Loop Road was designated a National Scenic Byway for good reason. The 32-mile drive packs in some of the most scenic vistas in all of New England, from the dramatic granite cliffs at Otter Point to the picturesque landscape of Jordan Pond to the all-encompassing views of the Atlantic from the summit of Cadillac Mountain. Fall is glorious here; a forest fire in 1947 burned much of the dominant evergreen forest on the eastern side of Mount Desert Island, allowing colorful northern hardwoods to take over the land. Plan to spend at least three hours to enjoy all of the scenery on this drive, and you'll find numerous other walks and hikes available at many points along the way. We have also outlined a second, optional loop drive that visits several other scenic spots on the island that are not accessible via the Park Loop Road. A detailed audio tour and trail map of the park are available at the Hulls Cove Visitor Center (visit www.nps.gov/acad/index.htm), where this trip starts. For more detailed hiking information, pick up a copy of our book *Discover Acadia National Park: A Guide to the Best Hiking, Biking, and Paddling.*

Basic Route: This trip follows the Park Loop Road for its entire length. Near the end of the trip, it follows the auto road up to the summit of Cadillac Mountain.

Start and Finish: Hulls Cove Visitor Center in Acadia National Park. The visitor center is located on ME 3, 2.5 miles north of Bar Harbor.

◉ **GPS coordinates:**
N 44 24.561, W 68 14.740.

Distance
32 miles round-trip with an optional 21-mile second loop.
Approximate Driving Time
1 hour 20 minutes
Peak Time
First and second weeks of October
Services
Bar Harbor
Fees
$20 per vehicle park entrance fee

🔺 This small mountain at Sand Beach, on the Ocean Drive section of the Park Loop Road, is known as the Beehive.

When you start the drive from the park's visitor center, you will immediately notice the beautiful granite stonework that adorns the bridges, culverts, and rest areas that are present throughout the drive. The granite, known as Cadillac granite, has a wonderful pink hue, and was quarried from various locations on the island. There are several excellent viewpoints of the islands in Frenchman Bay and the interior mountains during the first several miles of the drive At the 3-mile mark, be sure to turn left, following the sign to Sand Beach.

Hot Spot: Sieur de Monts Spring. About 5.8 miles from the visitor center, there is parking on the right for Sieur de Monts Spring. This area features a great walking trail through a forest of paper birch trees, as well as the Abbe Museum of Native American history, and the Wild Gardens of Acadia, a wonderful collection of native wildflowers and other plants growing in native habitats.

◉ **GPS coordinates:**
N 44 21.734, W 68 12.339.

Hot Spot: Sand Beach and Ocean Drive. Another 3 miles beyond Sieur de Monts is the most scenic coastal road in all of New England, Ocean Drive. At the north end of the drive is a parking area for Sand Beach, a stunningly beautiful 0.75-mile-long stretch of sand in a cove bordered by Cadillac granite cliffs on either side. Beyond Sand Beach, Ocean Drive parallels the coast along the edge of dramatic rock ledges interrupted by a pair of cobblestone beaches. You can park in the right lane the length of Ocean Drive, allowing you to pull over and take in the sights, sounds, and smell of the surf whenever you want. Worthwhile stopping points include Thunder Hole, Monument Cove, Otter Cliffs, and Otter Point.

GPS coordinates:
N 44 19.757, W 68 11.116.

Hot Spot: Jordan Pond. After Ocean Drive, the road follows the shoreline for a few more miles before heading inland, reaching Jordan Pond 6 miles beyond Otter Point. You can park at the Jordan Pond House or in a larger lot, about 0.25 mile past the main entrance. Tea and popovers on the lawn of the Jordan Pond House is

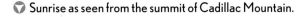

Sunrise as seen from the summit of Cadillac Mountain.

an Acadia tradition well worth the wait on a busy fall day. The lawn has a beautiful view of the pond and "the Bubbles," a pair of small rounded hills with bald summits. A loop hike around the pond takes about one and a half hours and is a great way to see the fall colors reflecting in the pond's waters.

Optional Second Loop Drive

Mount Desert Island is home to many scenic spots that the Park Loop Road doesn't visit. If you want to see more of the eastern side of the island, you can drive this loop from downtown Bar Harbor by following ME 3 south to ME 198 north in Northeast Harbor, to ME 233 near Somesville, back to Bar Harbor. Good spots to stop along the way include the Tarn (2.2 miles south of Bar Harbor), Seal Harbor beach (opposite the Jordan Pond entrance to the Park Loop Road), Little Long Pond (just beyond Seal Harbor beach), Asticou Azalea Garden (on ME 198, 0.2 mile from ME 3), and Eagle Lake (on ME 233, 2.1 miles west of Bar Harbor). Except for at the beach, there should be nice fall foliage at all of these locations. The loop is about 22 miles long and should take about 45 minutes to drive.

● **GPS coordinates:**
N 44 19.341, W 68 15.141.

Hot Spot: Cadillac Mountain Summit. Beyond Jordan Pond, the road will give you both an intimate look at the forest foliage and views out across the pond and Eagle Lake. For the really big views, turn right onto the Cadillac Mountain auto road, 4 miles from the Jordan Pond House. The auto road is about 4 miles long, passing views of the park, Frenchman Bay, and beyond at just about every turn. There is a large parking lot and gift shop on the summit, but obviously the real attraction is the views. At 1,522 feet above sea level, Cadillac is the highest point on the eastern seaboard, and sees the first light of day every morning. Watching the sunrise from the peak is another Acadia tradition that inspires several hundred people a day to get up early and make the drive or hike to the top. Bring an extra jacket, as the change in elevation and the exposed nature of the summit can make it a much chillier place than in the valleys below.

● **GPS coordinates:**
N 44 21.165, W 68 13.525.

To complete the trip, drive back down the auto road and turn right onto the Park Loop Road, following it about 4 miles to the visitor center. Alternatively, you can take ME 233 into Bar Harbor just past the turnoff for Sand Beach, about a mile after the Cadillac auto road.

Maine's Midcoast: Wiscasset to Camden

The Trip: The midcoast region of Maine is home to many of the characteristics that define Maine's state motto, "The way life should be." Every nook and cranny of this drive turns up working fishing harbors, lighthouses, dramatic coastline, and eclectic villages filled with art galleries, antiques shops, clam shacks, and quaint bistros. The drive starts in Wiscasset, which bills itself as the "Prettiest little town in Maine," and ends atop Mount Battie in Camden Hills State Park. In between, you will visit three lighthouses and be treated to views of rocky Atlantic shoreline and hillsides awash in fall colors. Brilliant orange and red maples can be found along the main streets and in the Camden Hills, while the shoreline part of the drive will feature the golden and russet tones of oaks and marsh grasses. Although the drive takes about three hours straight through, you will want to devote an entire day to this trip to take advantage of all it has to offer.

Basic Route: This trip follows US 1 from Wiscasset to Camden, but takes many detours on side roads that are too numerous to mention here. Follow the detailed driving instructions below.

Start: US 1 and ME 218 in downtown Wiscasset, Maine. Wiscasset has a short Main Street with plenty of shops and restaurants to explore. It is also worth walking the side roads (Water, Pleasant, Fort Hill, Middle) that lead down to the water.

◉ **GPS coordinates:**
N 44, 0.159, W 69 39.875.

Distance	
110 miles one-way	
Approximate Driving Time	
3 hours	
Peak Time	
Second and third weeks of October	
Services	
Wiscasset, Damariscotta, Waldoboro, Thomaston, Port Clyde, Rockland, Rockport, Camden	
Fees	
$4.50 per person for entrance to Camden Hills State Park	

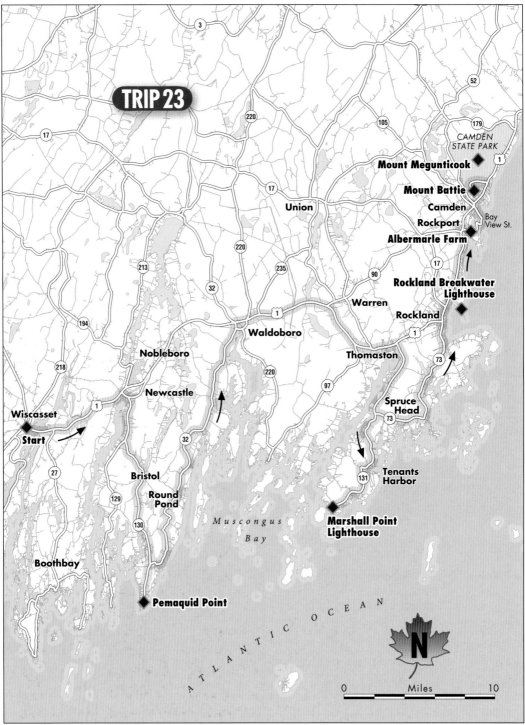

TRIP 23

3

52

220

17

105

179

CAMDEN
STATE PARK

Mount Megunticook

1

17

Mount Battie

Union

Camden

220

Rockport

Bay
View St.

Albermarle Farm

235

17

90

**Rockland Breakwater
Lighthouse**

213

Warren

32

194

1

Rockland

1

Waldoboro

73

218

Nobleboro

Thomaston

220

Newcastle

97

**Spruce
Head**

73

Wiscasset

Start

32

73

131

**Tenants
Harbor**

27

Bristol

129

**Round
Pond**

*Muscongus
Bay*

130

**Marshall Point
Lighthouse**

Boothbay

◆ **Pemaquid Point**

A T L A N T I C   O C E A N

N

0   Miles   10

Paul Woodward, © The Countryman Press

From Wiscasset, Follow US 1 east for 7.8 miles to Damariscotta, and turn right on ME 130 toward Pemaquid Point.

Hot Spot: Pemaquid Point Lighthouse. The 38-foot-high white tower of Pemaquid Point is one of the most photographed lighthouses in the state, as it is perched above deeply scored bedrock that dramatically slopes down to the water's edge. The lighthouse is usually open for tours from 10.30 to 5, Memorial Day through Columbus Day.

◉ **GPS coordinates:**
N 43 50.289, W 69 30.379.

From Pemaquid, head back north on ME 130 for 3 miles, turning right on ME 32 for a drive up the east side of the peninsula. You'll pass two interesting little harbors, New Harbor and Round Pond, where commercial fishing piers are bustling with activity and covered in lobster traps and buoys. About 20 miles from ME 130, ME 32 ends at US 1; turn right on US 1 for the relatively nondescript 12.5 miles to ME 131 in Thomaston. (If you want to extend the drive by another 45 minutes or so, you can make the drive to Friendship and back via ME 220 and ME 97.)

Hot Spot: Marshall Point Light, Port Clyde. At the end of ME 131, about 14 miles south of Thomaston, is Port Clyde, a little harbor with a restaurant and a shop or two that is best known for its ferry to Monhegan Island, and the Marshall Point Lighthouse. The 24-foot-tall black-and-white light was built in 1858 and is approached by a white wooden walkway that photographers just love. There is a museum adjacent to the lighthouse that is open from Memorial Day to Columbus Day. To get to the lighthouse, follow Drift Inn Road, just north of the harbor, to Marshall Point Road.

◉ **GPS coordinates:**
N 43 55.073, W 69 15.603.

From Port Clyde, drive north on ME 131 for about 9 miles, turning right on ME 73 in Tenants Harbor. ME 73 winds through forests and fields, passing classic Maine coast cedar-shingled homes and occasional views of the ocean, reaching US 1 in Rockland in 11 miles. Drive north on US 1 through Rockland, the biggest of the towns on this route. The downtown area has some great shops and restaurants.

Hot Spot: Breakwater Lighthouse, Rockland. On the northeastern edge of Rockland Harbor, a rock breakwater stretches for nearly a mile into the harbor. The red-brick lighthouse stands at the end of the breakwater, which has commanding views of Rockland Harbor and the nearby Camden Hills. The light is open to the public on weekends from Memorial Day through Columbus Day. To get to the breakwater from US 1, turn right on Waldo Avenue, about 1.5 miles north of ME 73, then turn right on Samoset Road and follow it until it ends at Breakwater Park.

⦿ GPS coordinates:
N 44 6.934, W 69 5.018.

From Rockland, follow US 1 north to Rockport, turning right on Pascale Avenue, 4.5 miles north of Waldo Avenue in Rockland. Follow Pascale through downtown (and past the memorial to André the Seal) to Main Street, turning right on Main and then making another quick right onto Central Street. About 100 yards later, turn right on Russell Avenue and drive past stone walls, seaside homes, and the Aldermere Farm, home to a herd of curious-looking Belted Galloway cows. At the Rockport cemetery turn right on Bayview Street and

▼ View of Camden, Maine, from summit of Mount Battie.

a 1.5-mile drive back to US 1 in downtown Camden. You will want to take a break in Camden, which has one of the most vibrant Main Streets on the Maine coast, and a beautiful harbor filled with sailing vessels of all makes and sizes.

Hot Spot: Camden Hills State Park. Continuing north on US 1 from Camden for 1.6 miles brings you to Camden Hills State Park, which provides some great hiking and camping opportunities, as well as the road to the summit of Mount Battie. Rising to 800 feet above sea level in less than a mile from Camden Harbor, the bald summit of Mount Battie has sweeping views of Camden, the harbor, and Penobscot Bay. Have your camera at the ready, as the steeples of Camden churches rising up from a sea of fall color is a favorite subject of Maine photographers and artists. This is a great place to end the trip and look over the entire route.

⬤ **GPS coordinates:**
N 44 13.365, W 69 4.139.

Mount Megunticook Leg Stretcher

If you'd rather not drive up Mount Battie, you can hike up the mountain in about 30 minutes via the Carriage Road Trail. If you prefer to enjoy the views without the noise of a parking lot, hike up to the Ocean Lookout on nearby Mount Megunticook. The Mount Megunticook Trail leaves the right side of the Mount Battie auto road, about 0.25 mile from the park entrance. The trail climbs steeply for much of the 1.4 miles to the lookout, where the views of Penobscot Bay are excellent. The trail continues for another 0.5 mile to the summit, but the trees hide the view there. The 2.8-mile round-trip should take about two hours.

⬤ **GPS coordinates:**
N 44 13.780, W 69 3.139.

TRIP 24

Rhode Island Beaches and Mansions: Westerly to Newport

The Trip: This route passes through more development than any other trip in this guide, but fall is a great time to explore the many miles of Rhode Island beaches on the state's southern shore as well as the historic and beautiful city of Newport. While you won't find the spectacular color of a northern New England fall along the beachfronts, you will find plenty of autumn color on the stretches of road that pass through marshes and farmland, and on the grounds of Newport's famous mansions. This trip has a definite nautical feel,

Distance
60 miles round-trip
Approximate Driving Time
2 hours
Peak Time
Third and fourth weeks of October
Services
Westerly, Watch Hill, Point Judith, Newport
Fees
$4 per car Pell Bridge toll

◀ Chase Farm, Saunderstown, Rhode Island

from the waterfront in Watch Hill to the Point Judith Lighthouse to the harbor in Newport, which was home to the America's Cup sailing race for nearly 100 years.

Basic Route: This trip follows US 1 and 1A east for about 18 miles from Westerly to Narragansett, with a side trip on Watch Hill Road to that small oceanside village. In Narragansett, the trip loops down to Point Judith and back on RI 108 and Ocean Road (1A), before heading to Newport on RI 138. Once across the Newport bridge (Pell Bridge), you will turn right on RI 138 to head into downtown Newport. Past downtown, the trip loops around the peninsula south of the city on a series of side streets and Bellevue Avenue, site of many of Newport's mansions.

Start: US 1 and US 1A in downtown Westerly, Rhode Island. Westerly is a small city on the Connecticut border with a vibrant downtown and attractive city park. To begin the trip, head south (east) on RI 1A.

⦿ **GPS coordinates:**
N 41 22.599, W 71 49.736

135

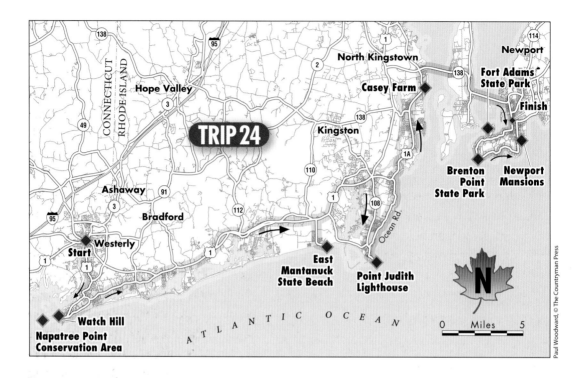

Paul Woodward, © The Countryman Press

Hot Spot: Watch Hill. South of Westerly 3.7 miles, go straight on Watch Hill Road where RI 1A turns left. About 2 miles later, you will reach Watch Hill, a summer beach community with a nice collection of shops and restaurants (many close after Columbus Day). The real highlight is the Napatree Point Conservation Area, accessible from a pair of parking lots on Bay Street. A walk next to the dunes on this mile-long spit of sand will give you views of the nearby Watch Hill Lighthouse. There is also the potential for some good birding here, as it is an important stopover point for migratory shorebirds.

⬤ **GPS coordinates:**
N 41 18.594, W 71 51.465.

From Watch Hill, head back to RI 1A and turn right, following it for about 5 miles to US 1 east, which will then take you another 16 miles to Narragansett. This roughly 20-mile stretch of Rhode Island shoreline features the state's best beaches, which are accessible from several roads on the right. One of our favorites is East Matunuck State Beach, which can be accessed by turning right on Matunuck Beach Road, about 11 miles east of RI 1A. The road to Matunuck passes by farms bordered by stone walls and extensive marshes, where you can spot wading birds like herons and egrets. The beach itself is popular with the surfing crowd.

Hot Spot: Point Judith Lighthouse. In Narragansett, turn right onto RI 108 and follow it for 4.7 miles to Ocean Road; turn right on Ocean Road for the 1-mile drive to Point Judith Lighthouse. While there is no foliage to speak of here, the light is in a beautiful spot, perched high up on the rocks at the end of the peninsula, waves crashing at its base.

● **GPS coordinates:**
N 41 21.697, W 71 28.839.

To get to Newport, drive back up Ocean Road to RI 108, but instead of taking that road, turn right onto the continuation of Ocean Road, which follows the water, passing Scarborough State Beach and the gift shops at Narragansett Pier as it becomes RI 1A.

Hot Spot: Casey Farm, Saunderstown. About 12 miles northeast of Point Judith is Casey Farm, a historic farm and homestead that dates back to the mid-18th century and is preserved by Historic New England. The farm currently raises organic vegetables and offers a guided tour ($4) of the farmyard and the old Casey family cemetery, where six generations of Caseys are buried. There are nice views from the farm across Narragansett Bay.

● **GPS coordinates:**
N 41 30.836, W 71 25.350.

About 1 mile north of Casey Farm, take the exit for RI 138 east, which will take you over two large bridges on the way to Newport. Once across the second bridge (Pell Bridge, $4 toll), take the Newport exit for RI 238 south.

Downtown Newport is in about 2.5 miles, with a public parking lot on the right, 2.7 miles south of RI 138. There is a lot to see and do (and eat) in Newport, so plan on giving yourself at least a couple of hours to walk the streets, some paved, some cobblestone. In the heart of downtown, you will see a sign for Ocean Drive. Turn right on Thames Street, and keep following the signs for Ocean Drive, following Wellington Avenue and Harrison Avenue west and south.

Newport Hot Spots:

Fort Adams State Park. About 2 miles after turning onto Thames Street, you will pass Fort Adams State Park on the right. Fort Adams is worth the visit for its grassy lawns and harbor views alone, but history buffs will also enjoy the historic fort buildings, which date back to 1824. Guided tours inside the fort are available Memorial Day through Columbus Day ($10 for adults, $5 for youth).

● **GPS coordinates:**
N 41 28.212, W 71 20.423.

Brenton Point State Park. Half a mile past Fort Adams State Park, turn right onto Ridge Road, which leads another 0.8 mile to Ocean Avenue; turn right on Ocean. You will soon see parking on the left and right for Brenton Point State Park, which provides access to the beautiful rocky shoreline of the peninsula.

◉ **GPS coordinates:**
N 41 26.977, W 71 21.331.

Bellevue Avenue. The 3.5-mile drive from Brenton Point to Bellevue Avenue hugs the coast in spectacular fashion, with the Atlantic Ocean on the right and beautiful large homes on the left. Once you turn right on Bellevue Avenue, however, you will find the famed mansions of Newport. With names like The Breakers, and Chateau-sur-Mer, these "cottages" date back to the mid- and late-19th century, and were the summer homes of some of America's wealthiest families, like the Vanderbilts and Astors. The mansions feature a beautiful array of architectural styles, from the Italian Renaissance–inspired 70-room palazzo that is the Breakers, to the high Victorian architecture of Chateau-sur-Mer, to the Vanderbilts' Marble House, inspired by Petit Trianon at Versailles. Today, nine of the mansions are preserved and managed by the Preservation Society of Newport County (www.newportmansions.org). The society offers a variety of admission options (tickets start at $12 for adults, $4.50 for kids) depending on how much time and how many mansions you want to visit.

◉ **GPS coordinates:**
N 41 28.317, W 71 18.458.

To return to downtown Newport, continue north on Bellevue Avenue to Memorial Boulevard (RI 138) and turn left.

Historic Seacoast: Newburyport, Massachusetts, to Ogunquit, Maine

The Trip: This route through some of New England's most historic coastline is great for late in the fall. When peak foliage has passed farther inland, the oak-hickory forests and salt marshes on the coast turn brilliant shades of gold, scarlet, and bronze.

Distance
45 miles one-way
Approximate Driving Time
1 hour 30 minutes
Peak Time
Third week of October
Services
Available along most of the route
Fees
$4 for adults, $2 for children for entrance to Odiorne Point State Park. There are also parking fees at all of the beaches along the route, and you may need to pay for parking in the cities of Newburyport and Portsmouth, and the village of Ogunquit.

The road hugs the Atlantic shoreline for many miles of this drive, so you will have crashing waves and clear blue waters on your right and beautiful salt marshes and forests on the left. The cities of Newburyport, Massachusetts, and Portsmouth, New Hampshire, have vibrant downtowns that are steeped in colonial history and architecture spanning three centuries. In addition, there are numerous beaches along the way, and you are never more than a few miles from a walk on the sand. Of course, this also means that sections of this drive are congested with beach houses and condos; Hampton Beach may be the most kitschy of all New England beach communities with its T-shirt shops and arcades. However, this is still one of the best coastal drives in New England, both for its scenery and its culture. Depending on how much time you spend in the towns, beaches, and parks, this trip will easily take half a day or more to complete.

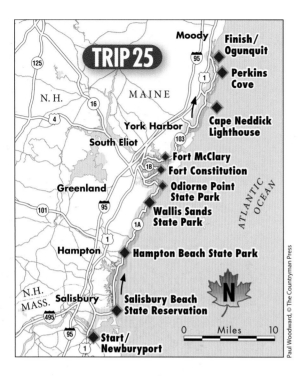

Paul Woodward, © The Countryman Press

Basic Route: This trip follows MA/NH 1A north from Newburyport to Portsmouth, with a detour to New Castle Island on NH 1B. It then follows US 1, ME 103, ME 1A, and Shore Road from Portsmouth to Ogunquit, Maine.

Start: Downtown Newburyport. Newburyport has all the trendy restaurants, art galleries, and shops one expects in a great New England coastal city, but what's notable about Newburyport is that it looks the part as well, with historic brick buildings mixing well with more modern architecture. The city is small and walkable, includes a nice wooden riverwalk, and is

close to perhaps the best beach walking in all of New England, on Plum Island. The center of town is at the intersection of State and Water streets, about 0.2 mile from US 1. To start the drive, head from downtown on Water Street to US 1 and turn right, in the direction of Salisbury and New Hampshire.

◉ **GPS coordinates:**
N 42 48.678, W 70 52.188.

A little over 2 miles north of Newburyport, turn right onto MA 1A (Beach Road), which reaches Salisbury Beach State Reservation (camping and beach access) in about 2 miles. This is also where you will get your first good look at the salt marshes that will be common from here to Portsmouth. Turn left to stay on 1A. The next 8 or 9 miles take you past the most congested beachfront property on this drive as you go through Salisbury, Seabrook, and Hampton Beach. Most of this section is less than scenic, but after North Hampton Beach State Park, the condos are replaced by long ocean views, stately mansions, and beautiful salt marshes.

Hot Spot: Odiorne Point State Park. The 8 miles after North Hampton Beach feature a succession of state parks and beaches: Jenness, Rye Harbor, Wallis Sands, and Odiorne Point. While Wallis Sands is our favorite of the beaches, Odiorne Point State Park is the most interesting, its 2 miles of undeveloped shoreline alternating between

🔺 Frost on grasses in a New Hampshire salt marsh.

rock ledges, cobblestone coves, and sandy beach. The park also has some unique history, being the first location in New Hampshire (in 1623) to see a European settlement and being home to a military fort during World War II. Several miles of trails explore the woods and shoreline of the park and New Hampshire Audubon runs a great natural-history center there—the Seacoast Science Center.

🔘 **GPS coordinates:**
N 43 2.637, W 70 42.987.

Hot Spot: New Castle. Continue on NH 1A north, turning right to stay on 1A at a traffic circle, 2 miles north of Odiorne. In another 0.5 mile, turn right onto NH 1B for a short detour to New Castle Island. As you cross the bridge to the island, you will pass Wentworth By the Sea, a historic hotel that was recently rescued from demolition and restored to its current state as a luxury hotel. Once on the island you will pass the Great Island Common on the right at 0.8 mile, which is an excellent spot for a picnic. On the eastern tip of the island overlooking the mouth of the Piscataqua River and the Atlantic Ocean, the view includes two lighthouses and the Isles of Shoals, a small island chain 6 miles offshore. Past the common at 0.4 mile, you will see a sign for Fort Constitution State Historic Site. This fort dates back to before the American Revolution and is still used to-

Replica of Captain Cook's *Endeavour* off Cape Neddick Lighthouse.

day as a U.S. Coast Guard Station. There is also a great view of the nearby Portsmouth Harbor Lighthouse.

◉ **GPS coordinates:**
N 43 3.915, W 70 42.999.

Continuing north on NH 1B eventually brings you into downtown Portsmouth, which, like Newburyport, features a diverse array of eclectic art galleries, shops, and restaurants. To get the full flavor of the city, you will want to find your way to Market Square (one block north of US 1 and US 1B) at the intersection of Market and Pleasant streets. For an in-depth look at the history of New Hampshire, visit Strawbery Banke, a living-history museum on Marcy Street.

NH 1B ends at State Street (US 1); turn right on State for the short drive over the Memorial Bridge to Kittery, Maine. About 0.5 mile beyond the bridge, turn right onto ME 103.

ME 103 winds its way through forest and across tidal creeks, passing through the little village of Kittery Point and past another historic fort worth a stop, Fort McClary, before ending at ME 1A in York Harbor, 9 miles from Portsmouth. Turn right on 1A for another beach drive, this time next to Long Sands Beach.

Hot Spot: Cape Neddick Lighthouse. At the end of Long Sands Beach turn right for the 1.2-mile drive to this oft-photographed lighthouse on an island, affectionately re-

Plum Island Leg Stretcher

If you head southeast on Water Street from downtown Newburyport, you will cross a bridge to Plum Island in 3 miles. Just after this bridge, turn right to enter the Harold Parker National Wildlife Refuge ($5 per car entrance fee). The road through the refuge passes sand dunes on the left and salt marshes and ponds on the right, which are important feeding grounds for shorebirds, wading birds, and a diverse mix of migrating waterfowl. Obviously, birders flock here, but beach lovers will enjoy walking the beach and dunes, which stretch for 6 miles without a house in site, from the refuge entrance south to Plum Island State Park. There are several beach-access points along the refuge road and at the state park. There is also a refuge visitor center located at 6 Plum Island Turnpike in Newburyport.

◉ **GPS coordinates:**
N 42 47.473, W 70 48.610.

ferred to as the Nubble. Its red and white buildings stand out beautifully against blue water and sky.

◉ GPS coordinates:
N 43 9.924, W 70 35.584.

Continue north on 1A through the hoopla of York Beach Village, then bear right onto Shore Road, about 1 mile beyond Nubble Road. Like most of this drive, Shore Road hugs the coast, providing great views of stately homes, tidal waters, and the open Atlantic.

Hot Spot: Perkins Cove, Ogunquit. Five miles beyond York Beach, turn right at Perkins Cove Road in Ogunquit. It is a short drive to Perkins Cove, where you will find a quaint harbor dotted with sailboats and lobster boats, and a fun collection of shops and restaurants. This is also the starting point for Marginal Way, a beautiful footpath that hugs the coast between Perkins Cove and the center of Ogunquit. Combined with the Oceanview Path, it makes a great 2-mile walk to Ogunquit Beach. You can also drive to the beach through the center of town by turning around and following Shore Road for 1 mile, turning right on Beach Street.

◉ GPS coordinates:
N 43 14.173, W 70 35.324.